project
YOU

INSPIRE · TRANSFORM · EMPOWER

MICHAEL ABDALLAH

All rights reserved. Except as permitted under the Australian Copyright Act 1968 (e.g., fair dealing for study, research, criticism or review), no part of this book may be reproduced, stored in a retrieval system, communicated or transmitted in any form or by any means without prior written permission from the author. All inquiries should be made to the author.

Cover design & layout (print and digital versions): Mélissa Caron
Editor: Richard Burian, MA, MLitt, CELTA

Publisher: Michael Abdallah, B.Sc.
Author: Michael Abdallah, B.Sc.

DISCLAIMER

The material in this publication is of the nature of general comment only and does not represent professional advice. It is not intended to provide specific guidance for particular circumstances and it should not be relied on as the basis for any decision to take action or not take action on any matter which it covers. Readers should obtain professional advice where appropriate, before making any such decision. To the maximum extent permitted by law, the author and publisher disclaim all responsibility and liability to any person, arising directly or indirectly from any person taking or not taking action based on the information in this publication.

ISBN: 978-0-646-82826-8

Subjects: Health mindset, Success mindset, Self-help, Self-discipline, Philosophy

MJM

This message is for three of the most amazing children that I have ever had the privilege of having in my life. I'll keep this short and try not to get too emotional as you all have had the most profound impact on my life. When each of you were born I realised that as much power as the word **'Love'** has, it doesn't give any justice to the feeling that is felt when you have a child.

No matter how rough your life ever gets, you keep standing! Because by standing strong and never running from any situation you'll always manage to find a way. No matter how rough those seas get you keep standing. No matter what, bubba, you never give up!

What matters to me is how well you are living, that you will not judge people, that you be kind to people, that you always show up early to whatever it is you have to do and that you make sure that you check your ego. Most importantly remember that it's never wrong to do the right thing because how you do **anything** will become how you do **everything**.

Lastly don't ever be afraid to fail, remember the only way to become successful in anything you desire means you'll need to take chances. If it means that you may fail, and fail again, then you keep failing until you figure out how to master whatever it is you desire.

Most people never reach their goal or achieve their dreams because they give up right before they were about to make it. There's a saying that I would always tell myself when at times I wasn't sure when or how I was going to make it, both personally and professionally, 'The darkest moment of the day is right before daybreak.' That saying has had the most profound impact on the way I handled my go through and I have no doubt it'll do the same for you.

Thomas Edison failed 10,000 times before he succeeded in creating that light bulb, yet when he was asked about his experience and perseverance he responded with this:

'I have not failed 10,000 times—
I've successfully found 10,000 ways that will not work.'

'I BELIEVE IN YOU'

table of contents

INTRODUCTION 11

    What happened to you was not fair! 15

CHAPTER 1: OUR ENVIRONMENT SHAPES OUR LIFE 19

    'Perceptions control your biology' 21

    Growth and Learning in the Uterus 22

    I Just Know 28

    What We See Isn't Always What We Think We See 32

    Reticular Activating System - *You'll Never Change Unless...'* 34

    The Biological Mind 37

    The Conscious Mind 38

    The Subconscious Mind 41

CHAPTER 2: CHANGE YOUR PERSPECTIVE
AND EVERYTHING CHANGES 47

    What Are E-Motions 52

    What is the Purpose of E-motions? 56

    What is Emotional Intelligence? 59

    Emotional Addictions 66

    How we encode Emotions 70

CHAPTER 3: BODYMIND 75

    Perception and Your Brain 80

    Bio-Electric Cells - *Cells: Out with the Old, in with the New* 84

    Placebo and Nocebo Paradox 89

    The Mind That Heals the Body 94

CHAPTER 4: ENERGY **99**

    The Thoughts Create Vibration and Frequency 106

    The Power of Words and Thoughts 109

    Habitual Vocabulary
    'Change your Words to change your World' 114

CHAPTER 5: THE HUMAN BRAIN **121**

    Experiencing vs. Remembering 126

    Understanding Brain Waves 131

    How the Brain learns - *'Implicit'* Vs. *'Explicit' Memories* 139

    Author's Message 143

CHAPTER 6: STRESS **147**

    How the Brain Performs Under Stress 152

    Good Stress vs. Bad Stress 153

    Anxiety 156

    Depression 163

    Order and Chaos 172

CHAPTER 7: THE FIRST PILLAR – MOVEMENT **177**

    Neurogenesis and Movement -
    'When your Body moves your Brain grooves' 182

    Movement and Mood 186

    Flexibility, Mobility and Pliability 189

    The Wisdom of Being Active and Not Exercising 194

    Vibration and Frequency of Movement 199

    Nutrient Assimilation and Toxin Elimination 203

    Calibrating Your Body 206

CHAPTER 8: THE SECOND PILLAR – NUTRITION ... 223

Emotional Eating and the Bliss Point Explained ... 228

Frequency Food ... 231

The No Diet Diet ... 234

Calories In Versus Calories Out
What Does That Even Mean? ... 236

Types Of Diets ... 239

Paleo ... 241

Veganism ... 243

Vegetarianism ... 247

Ketogenic Diet ... 248

Intermittent Fasting ... 252

CHAPTER 9: THE THIRD PILLAR – BREATHING ... 257

Breatharianism ... 263

Breathing For Weight Loss
'When you lose weight where does the weight go?' ... 270

Breathing Improves Cardiovascular Health ... 273

Breathing and Anxiety ... 276

So How Do I Breathe Better?
'Stress Causes Disruption To Our Breathing Patterns' ... 279

Breathing From Your Belly! ... 281

4-7-8 Breathing And The Vagus Nerve ... 282

CHAPTER 10: THE FOURTH PILLAR – HYDRATION ... 287

The Triple Point of Water ... 293

Water For Weight Loss ... 295

Dr Masuro Emoto ... 297

Water Memory ... 300

The Spirit of Water ... 304

CHAPTER 11: THE FIFTH PILLAR – SLEEP 313

Stages of Sleep 318

Sleep and Weight Loss
*'Sleep' is the missing transformational component
you've been looking for*.................................... 323

Why Can't We Sleep 326

Dreams... 329

How To Sleep Better 334

CHAPTER 12: THE SIXTH PILLAR – MINDFULNESS 339

The Mechanics of Meditation and the Benefits........ 341

What Is Consciousness? 344

How Do We Increase Our Awareness and Consciousness?. 352

Manifestation 357

Meditation Challenge 361

BRINGING IT ALL TOGETHER 365

Building Better Habits
Inch by Inch, Anything's a Cinch 371

Implementation Of Intention 377

ABOUT THE AUTHOR 382

APPENDIX A 389
BREAKOUT – Michael's Six Pillars Summary

APPENDIX B 395
Four-Week Fasting and Meal Plan Structure

APPENDIX C 398
Four-Week Food List

introduction

The most disheartening thing to hear anyone say is, *'I can't'*. It immediately makes me wonder what circumstances and situations have made this person lose belief in themselves and their abilities. The law of substitution says that 'What I tell myself is what I think about and what I focus on.' Truth is, all of our souls are here to heal, it's as simple as that. Rather than get all worked up and challenge your personal perceptions about your life and your surrounding environment by attempting to convince yourself that you are the most incredible and sophisticated of all of God's creations and capable of God-like qualities on this heavenly earth, I'd like to invite you to go on a journey and allow yourself to develop a better understanding about why it is you think, act and feel the way you do, and through this newfound self-empowerment you will finally meet yourself.

As I write this I can't help but get choked up as I too have had my fair share of pains and suffering. All I can say about that is that it's through these pains that I was able to heal. Because how do you truly know how great you are unless you've had to go through the different types of pains? **'A man who** *is born blind will never know the true meaning of darkness because he has never experienced the light.'* That's because you need to experience both sides of the spectrum to call yourself strong or knowledgeable or to even say that you know.

We don't gain strength from being strong; we can only create strength from weakness. Think about it, if you are already great then you can't become great. It's the same thing with strength, and so these pains help our souls to heal and grow. It's through these pockets of chaos and order that we develop a wisdom that can't be taught in any textbook or school. Ultimately, you become enlightened and virtuous when you can be subjected to pains and be tempted by dark intentions or dark reactions, but instead you choose to do the right thing.

Horace Mann wrote, *'if any man seeks for greatness, let him forget greatness and ask for truth and he will find both'.* So the journey you're about to embark on is to introduce you to yourself, by educating you with the 'objective truth' and empowering you with knowledge and wisdom, because there is a power in knowing and then doing. We need both knowledge and wisdom to make an impact. If you want to impact the ones you love most, then lead by example. If you consistently do that you'll no doubt grow your own influence.

I've always been told how being average was okay and was always criticised about thinking outside the boundaries of conventional wisdom. As I write this I can't help but be grateful to all those who imposed their insecurities on me and wanted me to fail so that they wouldn't have to succeed.

And so, like it did for me, your wisdom will come to you from the most unlikeliest of places. And if you ever hit rock bottom, then you'll also learn that that's one of the best places to set some solid foundations from. Rock bottom can also be the most influential source of motivation for you. And so I consciously set out to put all the pieces together in what's becoming an overwhelming puzzle in understanding why it is that certain experiences never seem to get better and somehow keep repeating themselves in our lives.

In this book I have chosen to reduce the content into bite sized pieces, so that you are able to digest it. This allows us the opportunity to reconnect when I write the extended version of this book and explain its content in greater detail. There is however a small favour that I ask, and that is that after you read this book the first time that you read it again. What you will find is that you will not only see something in the book you didn't see the first time, you'll also see something in yourself you didn't.

I personally feel blessed in being able to channel and present to you this eye opening and empowering book, because I believe it has the complete spectrum in helping you put all the pieces together in creating the new you. And so I'll leave you with this quote before you embark on your quest of becoming who you are destined to become.

Rumi, my favourite theologian and poet says, **'The womb is the place where the light enters you.'** What I'd like you to take from that quote is that there is not one single thing in your life that has, or that will happen to you that will be a waste. If you can reflect on every single crisis, every inch of difficulty or all of your joy filled moments through the eyes of this newfound wisdom that you will acquire, what you will realise is that every moment is showing up so that you become more of whom you were meant to be.

what happened to you was not fair!

We've all experienced some sort of trauma in life, some of us from our own mistakes, whilst others from unprocessed disappointments and suppressed emotions. Yet, we continue to ruminate and revisit that past experience and reproduce the same associated emotions to that experience even when we are not at fault. The truth is that in every situation there's a lesson that can actually be learnt. However, the healing process is our responsibility, because if it wasn't, then an unfair circumstance eventually becomes a life that's unlived.

> Healing is our responsibility because that unprocessed pain now gets taken out on everyone around us. How is it fair for us to do to others what others have done to us?

> Healing is our responsibility because if we want to have a pain-free and happier life, then how will that ever happen by sitting around and waiting for someone else to make our pain disappear? It'll only make us dependent, needy and bitter.

> Healing is our responsibility because we all have the power to heal ourselves, even if we have been led to believe that we don't.

> Healing is our responsibility because being uncomfortable is a sign that the place in life that we're currently in isn't doing us justice anymore.

> Healing is our responsibility because every great person that you've admired began with every odd against them and learned that whatever life threw at them was no match for their inner strength.

> Healing is our responsibility because healing is you saying 'NO' to being who you thought you were. You now become someone stronger, someone wiser, someone who is relentless.

When we heal, we now step onto the side of the people we aspire to be like. We're not only able to metabolise the pain and grow, we are now able to create real change in our lives and everyone around us. We are now able to pursue our dreams more freely, we are now able to handle whatever life throws at us, because we are self-efficient and self-assured. We are more willing to dare, risk, and dream of broader horizons, ones we never thought we'd reach.

So the next time someone else does something wrong that would usually affect you, that would usually make you sit around and wait for them to take the pain away, remember that the pain can only be undone by you, and can only be taken away by you. That's when you'll realise that the hurts you felt were the most valuable lessons of your life, that became the catalyst to creating a more significant and profound you. We are not meant to get through life unweathered and unscarred; those scars are the first signs of acquiring *'true wisdom'*. And that could only happen once you no longer have any emotions attached to a past experience or circumstance. Learning about yourself through this book won't guarantee that you'll never be hurt again, but it will change the way you respond and whether you treat the trauma as a tragedy or allow it to become the beginning of how the *'Victim became the Victor'*.

Thank you for choosing to go on this journey with me as every bit of information was delicately selected to challenge your past perceptions and progressively help you remove the limitations you've allowed your experiences and environment to impose on you. Again I would strongly suggest you re-read this a second time and then even a third, because you won't just see something in the book you didn't see the first time you read it, you will see something in yourself you missed as well. That's the power and beauty of this book. Just remember that we learn a greater deal about ourselves by what didn't go right in our lives, and that it's not your fault that your life's story took a different path to the one you expected. Your journey hasn't even ended. In fact how do you really know that it's even started until you've come out on the other side of that pain with something to say, with some profound shift? And when you do then nothing will ever hold you back, no one can ever tell you you're not good enough, only you have the power.

Now allow me to introduce you to yourself.

chapter 1:

our environment shapes our life

'Perceptions control your biology'

What if you weren't really a victim of your genetics and what if you had complete control of your life and the responsibility to create your ideal life?

As a matter of fact you do, and what you believe plays a large role in controlling the outcomes you experience in your life. This is because your perception controls your biology and how you see the world. It determines your behaviour, shapes your life and even changes your genetic expression.

This may be a little hard for you to initially believe and may challenge your perceptual reality. That's absolutely fine, as I have no doubt that by the end of the book you'll have a much better and clearer understanding about where you got your beliefs, how you've developed your perceptions and effectively why you keep recreating your exact same reality and why it is you continue to wear the same lens of perceptions that has kept you anchored in the past. The journey will help you figure out why it's been so hard to change your life, more importantly equip you with the tools to finally create the sustainable change you've always desired.

|||||||||||||||||||||||||||||||||||||||||||||||||||||

'The world exists as you perceive it.
It is not what you see,
but how you see it.
It is not what you hear,
but how you hear it.
It is not what you feel,
but how you feel it.'
~ Rumi

|||||||||||||||||||||||||||||||||||||||||||||||||||||

growth and learning in the uterus

Within the first 24 hours of conception, every bit of your genetic information is already present. The makeup of your hair, the colour of your eyes, the colour of your skin, even the changes that your body goes through are all in this microscopic cell.

Once this cell has uploaded all of its DNA, it then splits into two new cells in a process known as 'Mitosis'. Now each new cell receives a complete copy of all the DNA data. By the fourth week of being inside the mother's womb you have developed into a small being that grows at a rate of one million cells per second. In the second month of our development our heart starts to beat and our brains now grow at a rate of 100,000 cells per minute. The second month of our development is where we start to become affected by our mother's beliefs, her habits, her insecurities and worse, her emotional turbulence and instabilities.

By the third month our ears start forming and is when we start hearing our mother's heartbeat and voice; in this month we begin developing our movement. By the fourth month we now start to develop our taste buds and learn to appreciate certain foods and flavours. For example, an Indian baby begins appreciating spicy food. This process is referred to as 'Foetal Programming', also known as 'Parental Programming'. This theory suggests that the environment that surrounds the foetus during its development plays a significant role in determining the risk of disease, obesity and cognitive dysfunction, and to some extent even character. The theory goes on to state that the environment of the foetus is controlled by the mental, physical and emotional health of the mother, including her lifestyle choices and belief system.

During months five through to eight we go through pretty impressive growth spurts. We start to develop our expressions, as well as learn emotions and language. This growth spurt is also why we immediately have a preference for the language of our parents when we're born. We spend most of our time sleeping during these months. That's because when we're asleep, the brain emits theta waves (which are the gateway to the subconscious mind). When the brain emits theta waves you're in hypnosis mode and effectively where you developed your automatic programs known as your *'habits and behaviours'*. I highlight these facts for the sole purpose of pointing out how we actually begin to learn and develop our habits and behaviours even before we're born; and that they are largely influenced initially by our mother and later on by our environment. All this, we will explore throughout this chapter.

In the last month of this process you now begin to practice your motor skills and the puzzle between nurture and nature is now underway. This is the month you start showing the first image of the character you've been developing over the last nine months. The truth is that a baby effectively learns about the world through the mother's experiences and her responses to her environment. The chemistry from the mother's brain to the cells that organises her body also affects and impacts the cells and chemistry in the foetus. The foetus learns through emotions and the beliefs of the mother; the baby is learning the emotional chemistry to the habits and behaviours of what becomes the unconscious default program of the baby when it is born.

I get that you may be thinking how this is even possible, especially if you go by the scholastic model of the '80s and '90s, where it was thought and taught that the baby's brain and foetus don't really have any real significant function until just before the baby is born. So here is a question for you: What does your doctor get you to do when he or she wants to work out what your hormones and stress levels are like? A blood test, right? The point is that if the same blood passes through the placenta is passing through the umbilical cord with the sole purpose of delivering nutrients and keeping that baby alive, then can it be possible that the hormonal imbalances and biological stresses that affect the mother also affect the baby?

Epigenetics now demonstrates that that's exactly the case and that if the mother is stressed and angry, the baby too will experience being stressed and angry. Equally, if the mother is happy then the chemical changes the body goes through that are responsible for making the mother happy will make the baby experience being happy. In short, the emotional patterns and behaviours of the mother are being learned by the baby before it's born. But more importantly, science is now starting to show how the parenting style of a mother can also affect the baby's genes. The child's development phase does not stop there. The next 12 years are so crucial in how the child develops both its intrinsic and extrinsic belief systems, and how they impact the child's biology, physiology, neurochemistry, neurology, and more importantly, what that child becomes and attracts in their life.

So why is the influence of the mother so important in the development of the foetus to a baby and then child? It's so the baby is prepared for the world that lies ahead. Think of yourself as an iPhone for a moment. When you first unpack the iPhone it comes with its default programs, so that you and your phone are able to communicate and connect. Throughout your time with your iPhone you are then able to individualise and tailor-make it to suit your personal tastes and requirements by adding the apps and programs that resonate with your current belief systems. The default program, however, was necessary to start you off in being able to understand the phone. It's comparable to being a child of our parents. Without this unconscious download of genetic information from our parents, we would just be numb and not know how to take in our environment or interact with it. Throughout our life we may change or adapt our belief systems. The journey of our lives is us adding or removing the 'programs' that are relevant to what we believe to be true at the time.

The issue is you may have been taught all the belief systems and programs you don't want in life. Throughout the coming chapters you should expect to appreciate both the significance and the impact your parents' belief system has had on your general attitude, as well as how your socioemotional development has shaped most of your outlook and perceptions in life. This is why most therapists will trace your unconscious behavioural patterns to when you were a child. We will explore how we develop, and most importantly, how we can finally create sustainable change and finally close the gap between how we appear and who we really desire to be in life.

I just know

Before we begin to delve into the depths of how our cells are largely influenced by how we think, how we act and how we feel, a quick explanation is required about the biological systems the body puts in place to keep us streamlined to survive. These systems collect all our data and they design the programs that continually redefine our lives. Those same systems are what have allowed us to evolve and stand the test of time. In our initial years we develop a belief system that is referred to as the 'cognitive bias', which now starts to shape our reality. It has been said that cognitive bias is the biggest self-imposed obstacle to progress, not just to ourselves, but to all of mankind.

We are wired to make cognitive shortcuts; those shortcuts become our base or default program.

The longer we keep running those programs the more embedded they become into our DNA and eventually shape who we are and who we become. You can almost say that those belief systems and programs end up shaping our personal reality that we call life.

These shortcuts effectively become intrinsic biases, which are subconscious stereotypes that affect the way we make decisions. They stem from the societal cues we have been receiving throughout our entire lives, for example, our parents, or our communities and especially our schools and teachers. We are for the most part completely unaware of these biases. However, they have a profound impact on the way we function and how we perceive a situation to be and what information we choose to believe.

Which then becomes a great source of tragedy as we sincerely believe that we actually see the world as it is and that the rest of the world is deluded and maybe even impervious to logic ('our logic'). Yet, on the other side of that fence, you have someone else looking at you in the same manner and believing their opposing views to yours about themselves and the world around them.

This pattern and way of thinking transfers right throughout our entire world, and existential system, it doesn't just stop with our parents. Look at our schooling system. The information that is taught to us is the content that was decided by the teacher, the curriculum, or an institution, which now gives rise for that same bias that you've developed unconsciously to dictate the translation and content taught, ultimately resulting in a distorted truth in the information conclusion.

The information is distorted by the process of selection of what information the teacher deemed important at that time that was relevant to his or her perceptions and that the information translated to you is now information that may be omitting the information that could've been utilised by you for your future and successes.

The schooling system with their stick and carrot reward system is designed to discourage any deviation from its prescribed path and as a result we adopted this passive acceptance of all its information and never questioned it. It's easier that way, and even worse, it involves absolutely no effort of independent thought, which has now become the new norm and habit for most of mankind.

This habitual pattern becomes disastrous later on in our lives, because we find ourselves now just accepting and conforming to the life we're told that we should have. These biases control everything, from the way we think to how we act. The reason for such a broad spectrum of possibilities in individual perceptions is that each individual tends to intuitively and unconsciously discard any information that goes against their preconceived ideals; because we tend to only gather and only believe in the information that supports our preconceived ideas.

Even though we are capable of so much more, we've been streamlined to be energy efficient to give us the best possible chance to survive. Our brains will take in everything but only run the information that fits in with our model to keep us using less fuel. The problem here is, who and what helped design the model that defines our reality? Who or what was passing down their perceptions, their biases, and their expectations? These influence our beliefs: if we can't do something, then why try? As a result we've become overstimulated with the limiting beliefs of what we can't achieve rather than what we can if we tried and embraced the opportunity to fail as a means to grow. So my question to you is, isn't it about time you created a life that resonates with you? A life that's effectively unique to you?

what we see isn't always what we think we see

Dr Daniel Simon is a cognitive psychologist and was investigating a phenomenon known as 'sustained inattentional blindness', which is basically a fancy way of saying 'perceptual blindness' where he exposes the illusion of memory. Or should I say the illusion of 'perceptual memory', which is where we think we perceive and remember more than what we actually do.

The test was referred to as the 'gorilla test' and became an internet sensation. In the test they had two groups of three people, one group wearing white shirts and the other group wearing black shirts. Each team had their own ball and were instructed to pass the ball to a member of their designated team. The subjects were now asked to count how many passes were made by the team wearing white shirts. The answer was 15 passes. The majority of the subjects were pleased as they got the answer right. But then they were asked, *'did you see the gorilla?'*

As you can imagine most thought it was a joke and said of course they had not. The subjects were then asked to watch the video again and this time not to count how many times the ball was being passed and sure enough, about one minute into watching the video the gorilla waltzes in between both teams passing the ball, pauses in the middle of the screen, beats his chest then waltzes back off. The whole thing takes about nine seconds.

I thought this was such a compelling illustration of the illusion of perceptual memory. We do not see the world as it is, but as we are. The results were clear. A man dressed up in a gorilla suit strolls along right in front of you, does a little dance and then walks off and you don't notice it. Yet we by nature intuitively believe that if we focus on a subject that our attention will automatically allow us to focus on that subject. The truth is that what we usually end up focussing on is what we believe matters to us. The best thing in all of this is that when you're able to use all this information you're acquiring to hone in on a life that you truly desire, then your world will literally become an extension of your mind. So don't be discouraged if your life hasn't panned out how you've hoped so far.

You see we consciously tend to notice things that we focus our attention on; we're all so confident that when something unexpected or distinctive happens right in front of us that we'll automatically see it. So if science has now reasoned that our conscious perceptions, that our conscious awareness is limited to what we focus on, then can it be possible that our current belief system alters the truth? Is it possible that what we see in a circumstance suits our preferences and the preferences of those belief systems?

reticular activating system

'You'll never change unless...'

'What you think about you bring about.' That's not just a metaphysical statement, it's now recognised by science as demonstrable. There's a part of your brain known as the 'reticular activating system' (RAS) and that's what teaches your brain what to

notice. There's the classic example of the car you've just bought. Once you bought that model or colour of car, you now suddenly seem to see them everywhere. So you ask yourself, *were there always that many cars like that there?* Inevitably you'll realise that of course there was, you just didn't notice them. That's because you decided (probably subconsciously) that this information wasn't important or notable, so your RAS didn't notice similar cars until you bought that car. That's when your brain said, 'Hey, this now important!' And as a result you're now noticing that particular car everywhere.

The reticular activating system is a network of neurons in the brain stem, which is also the seat to your subconscious mind and its primary job is to filter information and only allow the information that resonates with your current beliefs in. It will block out the rest.

Our brains are capable of incredible things, and the way the brain cells communicate is via a synaptic connection. The amazing thing is that the synaptic firing rate of the human brain is approximately 200 times per second, which results in *17.2 trillion action potentials*. Can you imagine if our brain took in all this information as though it were all of equal importance? It would literally go into a meltdown mode, so the RAS acts like a bouncer at a nightclub and only allows the information in according to what we perceive to be important. And this is why we usually only take in approximately 2000 bits of data per second.

This system is designed to protect your brain by filtering the information you let in to be the information that you agree with. Now, guess who programmed the filter to what information to block and what information to allow? You did! So if you start the day saying you'll never have the body you desire or you'll be overweight the rest of your life, your reticular activating system will go through the day highlighting everything that confirms those negative beliefs. Equally, if you tell yourself you're not good enough, your reticular activating system will look for all the evidence and confirm that belief all day long.

This may be one of the reasons we have a difficult time changing how we look and feel about ourselves.

The RAS is the reason behind when you learn a new word and then start hearing it everywhere.

It's the reason why you can tune in out a crowd full of talking people, yet immediately snap yourself back to the attention of someone who says your name or something that at least sounds like it.

the biological mind

The biological mind controls our biology, our behaviour and our genetics. The science of 'epigenetics' is a science of how an organism's perception of its environment can effectively modify and select its gene readout to reflect the belief in the perception. Chapter 3 is where we explore this phenomenon in depth.

Let's assume that in your environment you have a belief of being threatened, then your biology will provide a complimentary behaviour and release a reaction to suit that belief. Or if your belief is that of a world that is filled with joy and love and you genuinely believe that, then what will be released into your body is a chemistry that will also manifest the physical experience of that belief.

The function of the brain is to take our belief system and create a biological response equal to that belief and the function of the mind is to create coherence between what we believe and what we experience. When you're having positive thoughts, you're using your mind, which now influences your biology. However, there are two minds that we will elaborate on that are significant in understanding why we at times find it hard to change. They are completely unique in the way they operate and function. There is the conscious mind and that is referred to as our *'creative mind'* and then we have our **subconscious mind** which is better known as our *'habitual mind'*.

the conscious mind

The conscious mind absorbs information, transforms it into knowledge and then takes this newfound or recurring knowledge and produces the correlating action. Our conscious mind is extremely important as it allows us to process all the data that comes in via any of our 'subjective environmental experiences', which then in turn allows the subconscious to scan its inventory of *'habitual patterns'* also known as reactions. It will then apply the most relevant one to suit the perceived experience. Think of it as a relay system of our subconscious; it continually feeds new data into the subconscious mind.

I am sure that to some degree, you've heard so much about the conscious and subconscious mind, and yet you're still not entirely sure how they function, what roles they play and why they are so important. These explanations are intentionally oversimplified but are very relevant and all that is needed to be understood in order to process and understand how it is that we can change. The conscious mind is creative, it is able to think into the future or it can revisit the past. It is made up of all your wishes, your desires and aspirations. Sigmund Freud stated in his psychoanalytic theory of the personality, that the conscious mind consists of everything inside of our awareness and that it's the aspect of our mental processing that we can think and talk about in a rational way.

It's referred to as the creative mind as it is not bound by time. We're constantly either thinking of the future event or revisiting a past experience. For example, say you were scheduled to jump out of a plane tomorrow and it was your first time and you were nervous, you would literally start to live the moment as though the event is taking place right now. As you visualise the process of the jump, the body will begin to release the relevant chemical reaction making that jump feel real. For example, your palms would get sweaty and your heart would start to race with some level of nervousness. Equally, if a friend of yours called you and reminded you of a past experience, whether it be positive or negative, you would also start to relive that event as though it was happening right now. Your body would begin to produce the same biochemical changes that you experienced when that event took place.

In short, the conscious mind consists of everything inside our awareness, which includes things like our sensations, perceptions, memories and feelings. The main role of the conscious mind is to identify all of the incoming information. It is the analytical mind and is always evaluating right from wrong, positive from negative, which is made up of all your 'current perceptual reasoning', which now nurture your creative abilities, your will and your faith. (I say current because that can change throughout the journey of our lives. What we deem right or wrong may change based on a new belief system we've adopted at any time).

the subconscious mind

The 'subconscious mind' is a million times more powerful than the conscious mind. By that I mean the subconscious is the powerhouse of the mind. It can override and influence the conscious mind if it needs to. If our conscious choices, desires and aspirations are constantly changing, imagine how much energy the body and brain would be expending, always having to readjust, being that the body's primary job is to keep you alive? The habitual factual mind must have the final say and run what has been proven to be your preferred program and one that it recognises, all in the name of conserving energy, so that you can deal with any potential environmental threats. The subconscious mind lives in the present moment and does not look into the future nor does it reflect on the past like the 'conscious mind'. Its primary focus is to keep you alive and recognise all of your preferred personal habits and behaviours. It then applies them to respond to the stimuli that you're presented with. Your subconscious mind has what is called a homeostatic impulse. Besides, being your habitual mind (which means it tends to repeat your favoured and preferred habits), it also regulates your body's temperature and your breathing, it keeps your heart beating at a certain rate, it unconsciously regulates balance in all of the biochemicals in your entire body and streamlines you to remain functioning. Think about it, if you consciously had to focus on keeping your heart beating or had to focus on breathing in order to stay alive, it would be fair to say that life wouldn't be fun, as you would no doubt have to invest all your time in staying alive.

The subconscious mind makes up 95 percent of who you are, as it consists of both the positive and negative identifications you've associated yourself with. These have helped form your habits and behaviours, which were created by whatever your current belief system was. The reasoning behind emphasising the differences between the conscious and subconscious minds is because many people believe in their hearts and minds that they lead their lives based on their wishes and desires. For example, they wish to be happy and healthy, so that becomes their conscious intention. Initially they think they've worked it all out as everything seems to be making sense, but then the inevitable happens and they experience some level of turbulence and they now have a difficult time acquiring certain wishes, aspirations and desires in life.

Most people would immediately put the onus on 'fate' or that it's 'not the right time' or that the 'universe has different plans and isn't supporting me', which to some degree are all relevant. However, the major reason why is that although the conscious mind has those wishes and desires neuroscience studies show that we only operate from our **conscious** minds 5% of the day and the remaining 95% of the time we operate from our **subconscious** programs. Due to the fact that when the conscious mind is too busy paying attention to a past experience or a future thought it loses track of what's happening in the present moment. That's when the subconscious mind takes over and runs one of the programs based on your belief system and habits.

The subconscious deemed that they were important and fast tracked that behavioural pattern as your preferred action so that you would not have to think and waste energy in trying to figure out the best way to respond to any one of your situations. Here's a simple example of how we may overreact based on a perception, you have a conversation with a friend and they say a word that triggers a reaction. You might then believe that they are having a dig at you, so now your subconscious produces the behaviour of a person that responds with some level of agitation.

Your friend asks you if you're okay. You might then apologise and suggest that you thought they were having a go at you. In response, your friend might reassure you that this isn't the case. You overreacted based on a past perception, which saw you meet that experience with an expectation that was based on your past experience. And so the subconscious mind produced the relevant response to that perception.

Another example. You're now driving to work on the same road you would usually drive on in the same expected traffic. You have gone into deep thought about a future desire or maybe a past experience. The drive now becomes a blur, yet you still manage to reach your destination 20 minutes later. You then say to yourself, 'wow, I don't even remember getting here!' The point of this example is that as your conscious mind was consumed with playing out that past experience or future event the subconscious took over and drove you to the destination in its familiar path that it had recognised over the times you took that same route to work.

In short the subconscious mind is the enforcer of the conscious habits that were repeated until they no longer needed a thought to activate the program and are now on autopilot. Which proves the point that when you operate from the subconscious mind that you're unaware of having to choose those behaviours. It's called subconscious, 'Sub' meaning below consciousness. So if you have a belief system that says you're not good enough, or that you're not worthy of something then what do you think your program in life will reflect?

The final point I make here is that your life isn't a printout of your conscious wishes and desires but rather a printout of the subconscious programs you repeatedly run.

chapter 2:
change your perspective and everything changes

Your biology, physiology and your genetic expression are effectively controlled by your beliefs, behaviours, emotions and your environment. So, it would make perfect sense that if you changed the way you thought, felt and acted, you could improve your biology, your physiology, your biochemistry and more importantly improve your circumstances and how you process your environment and what you attract in your life.

Most people genuinely want to change, so they'll sign up to a self-help program, read a couple books, recite positive affirmations, and start the day by thinking positively. Yet they might still feel negative and sooner or later adversity sets in. Either that, or variables present themselves and people will revert back to bad habits. That may be a process you have experienced and are not sure why or how to break through the invisible barriers. These barriers keep us anchored in the cycle of setbacks. If you feel as though that may be the case for you then don't worry because you'll have all the information needed to help you make sense of all the self-sabotaging moments that are deeply embedded into your subconscious; and most importantly the tools to finally create sustainable change.

As we have established, *your mind is effectively your brain in action.* Your brain is where the data of all your thoughts and experiences is stored and also where all the wiring of your repeated habits are located. This leaves the question then, where are all your emotions stored? We don't have an external storage unit for our thoughts like an iCloud.

Candice Pert wrote a book called *'The Body is the Subconscious Mind'* where she addressed these questions. Sigmund Freud also wrote about this in his book called, *'The Subconscious'*, basically saying that your emotions are stored in the body as is your subconscious mind. Let's battle test this, whenever you think of a past experience that has had a profound impact on you, that you still haven't processed, doesn't your body literally start to react as though that experience is happening to you right now? If at that time that experience made you feel anxious or upset you would again begin to become flustered and feel overwhelmed. So now you're reliving the past experience as though that experience is happening right in the present. It's not easy to move past scars, especially if you've been hard done by. But you can't continue to hold yourself and life back by allowing yourself to be the victim of the past experience. But if you can change your perspective then in that moment everything else will begin to change and here's why, your perspective creates your perception and by that I mean the way you look at an object or a circumstance changes what you see in that object or circumstance. So perspective creates perception, your perception now creates a certain belief, that belief creates a behaviour. That specific behaviour creates an experience and finally that experience now creates a certain reality which now inevitably continues to reinforce the perspective.

So if you can teach yourself to change your perspective then in that exact same moment everything else changes. If it sounds simple, it's because it actually is that simple. However, the process of changing the belief system that you've associated all your beliefs with is the challenge. But if you continue to trust this process and allow it to challenge your current beliefs and change your perspective then there will come a time where you will eventually redefine the lens that's been shaping reality. Please remember this isn't a race, so don't overwhelm yourself and just go at a pace that feels right to you.

what are e-motions

||||||||||||||||||||||||||||||||||||||||||||||||||||||||

At the core of every stress,
every ache and pain,
and at the core of every dis-ease that
you may experience are e-motions.

||||||||||||||||||||||||||||||||||||||||||||||||||||||||

The emotions, memories and any undigested traumatic perceptions get buried deep in our subconscious and when they get triggered, our body reacts negatively. When we react, we react as though the past memories and trauma are happening right now; we are unable to adapt in the present moment.

Whenever we're dealt a traumatic experience that impacts us with overwhelming emotions, the body has this innate ability of releasing specific protective mechanisms that help us overcome and survive these traumatic experiences. This innate protective process suppresses these e-motions into our body, our 'BodyMind'. If you don't believe me then the next time you are faced with any overwhelming traumatic experience or you happen to get triggered into revisiting a past experience, look for muscular tension. For example, your knees tightening up or neck tension. Muscle tension is the first sign of this process.

So how is this possible? To keep this relatively simplified there are two parts to this answer. The first is that the human body is made of energy; you may appear to be solid, but if you were to be magnified many million times you'd see you were composed of atoms. This information isn't revolutionary as science tells us that all matter is made up of atoms and all atoms are basically energy. So we essentially are beings of pure energy.

The second part to this nuance is the word emotion broken down. 'E' stands for energy, added to the word 'motion'. So it basically means 'energy' in 'motion', which makes perfect sense that they at any time can feed into each other as they originate from the same source *'Energy'*. Emotions are extremely important to help us prepare for an action. Our actions are usually dictated by the way we feel and this is why it is super important that we allow ourselves to connect with whatever information our emotions are expressing, so that the most appropriate and relevant actions are taken that best deal with that event or circumstance.

When we feel any one of our emotions what we are really feeling is energy that vibrates at a certain frequency relevant to the level of intensity of that emotion. For example, anger or fear will vibrate at a different frequency to love or joy, we then physically take on the energy of the emotions that we feel. When the emotions are overwhelming and too powerful for us they then become stuck in our bodies.

Ancient Chinese medicine teaches that when the body starts learning the feelings of any emotion those emotions affect specific body parts. For example 'anger, bitterness, guilt and resentment' affect the liver. Which is why when a person drinks excessively they tend to become any one of those emotions that are trapped in that part of the body, as alcohol is known to impact the liver. It is also why people tend to get heated and angry when they are drunk.

The challenge is to get your head around the fact that anywhere in the body that you feel any sort of sensation or tension, is evidence that you are storing emotions from the past. When you continue to ruminate and replay any past traumatic experience, so that the biochemical responses to the e-motion do not continue to overwhelm you and suck the life force right out of you, your nervous system will then download those e-motions into a specific body part so that you can continue to function without the setback of dealing with the emotions of those traumatic experiences.

Our evolutionary programming has streamlined us to survive and stay alive by moving away from things that don't feel good to us and so any emotions that overwhelm us are now swept under the rug so they can be dealt with at a later stage. That way they don't hold us back. The issue is when we unconsciously and habitually do this, then these emotions will inevitably build up internally and cause some level of havoc in our lives. This eventually sees us attempting to make sense of things by looking at our external stimuli and environment for the answers to how these suppressed emotions are making us feel. However, we will never quite find the answers. That's because the answers we seek are inside us.

The message here is that your *biology is your biography* and that it is recreating itself all the time. It's also that the vast majority of the energy you expend every day is actually being used up to suppress the already suppressed e-motions (so that they don't overwhelm you and render you unable to deal with your day ahead or any potential environmental threats), and is why you may continuously feel sick, tired and lethargic. When you finally release the suppressed emotions you'll have access to all that energy and be able to use that to better yourself and life.

what is the purpose of e-motions?

Human beings have developed emotions over time; emotions have been a vital part of our survival. We are capable of some extraordinary and extreme levels of emotions. Take the example of love or hate, which are complete polar opposites. Yet, when those emotions are expressed in their extremes, they can either wreak havoc in a situation or can equally intensify a sensation and become empowering and uplifting. How we interpret these emotions is always governed by our past experiences and in-experiences.

When our ancestors first came into existence, our brains were wired to seek out pleasure with what is referred to as our *pleasure-seeking instincts*. Things like seeking out sex or hunting for food became some of the experiences that helped form the foundations to our subconsciously *intuitive primitive programs* and essential for the survival of mankind and our evolutionary process. The earliest emotions that we developed began with fear and then all the subsequent emotions were developed until we finally got to love and passion. All these emotions highlighted our *likes* and *dislikes*, which helped us to determine what to look for and what to steer clear of and is how they became crucial for our survival.

Our brains continued to develop throughout the process of our evolution, starting off with what's referred to as our **'reptilian brain'** which is our fight or flight autopilot. Next was our **'mammalian brain'** also known as our limbic or emotional brain, and is where we encode our memories, habits and emotions. Lastly, our newest brain is **'the neocortex'** which is the analytical part of the brain that rationalises and reasons. This process of development allowed us to eventually place labels to these emotions, for example, love, joy, hate, anger; but more importantly, to interpret them.

The brain basically evolved from the inside out and the reasons why emotions are extremely important is that they provided us with valuable insight and information to whatever event or circumstance we experienced whether it was past, present or future. They helped highlight the significance in the situation, e.g., anger usually tells us some boundary of ours has been violated. Or if you're experiencing the emotions of love, then that tells you that you could be in the presence of someone or something that's highly valued.

The adopted mentality such as 'suck it up', or 'boys don't cry' has seen us progressively lose touch with our emotions and suppress them until we feel like we're losing control. If your capacity to hold things in was likened to a cup then eventually that cup would overfill and spill out. When it does, that's when things get out of control and it might feel like they never seem to get better. As a result we might feel depressed, anxious and overwhelmed. The unfortunate thing is that this unspoken adopted attitude has seen us lose touch with our emotions and all the valuable information our emotions provide. The consequence is rendering us unable to cope with life and our environment as well as we could be, seeing us be overreactive and destructive.

what is emotional intelligence?

I disagree with those who say that IQ (intelligence) and EQ (emotional intelligence) are different. However, I would like to elaborate on the importance of having emotional intelligence or what I call 'emotional awareness'.

I strongly believe that emotional intelligence is not an entity apart from your intelligence but rather a unique intersection between your emotions and your intelligence. This includes what your feelings are, and the use of those feelings to make good decisions. It's being able to manage how you deal with stressful situations and control impulses. It's having the ability to stay motivated and optimistic when things don't exactly go how you've planned them to.

It's being able to read your social environment and empathise with how people may or may not be feeling. It's really a mixed bag of lollies and there really isn't a perfect explanation or a definitive description of what emotional intelligence is, as I feel that the ideal of its description will alter from person to person and the perceptions that they may have in life.

There's an area in your brain between your emotional and rational brain that's highly responsive to change, and the neurons between the emotional and rational parts of the brain form new synaptic connections, which means it's now creating a new program. The more you replay or reinforce the necessity for that specific program, the stronger those synaptic connections become.

I wanted to introduce this paragraph to prepare you for a more in-depth discussion and analysis about how we form our new programs and how they effectively become an extension of who we are and who we become in later chapters. Basically however, the emotional intelligence umbrella is made of four parts, which are:

1. Social awareness
2. Emotional social awareness
3. Self-management
4. Relationship management

There's a scene in the movie *The Blind Side* starring Sandra Bullock who played the character of a strong-willed Christian woman named Leigh Anne. The story was about a homeless African American teen by the name of Michael who has drifted in and out of the school system for years. Leigh Anne and her husband take him in. They eventually become his legal guardians; it ends up transforming both their lives. His tremendous size and protective instincts made him a formidable force on the gridiron, which was largely due to how the game was evolving.

It's genuinely a fantastic movie, in one particular scene Leigh Anne and her family were at an intersection and the night was cold and raining heavily. Leigh Anne glances over to her left and spots Michael walking in just a shirt and shorts freezing and says out loud, 'What's he wearing? It's freezing, what's his name again?' Her son in the back yells out, 'Big Mike!' She now looks all concerned and says to herself, 'Where is he going?'

Her husband Sean pulls the window down and asks, 'Hey, big Mike, where ya headin'?'
'Gym,' replies Big Mike, while he's still rubbing his arms trying to stay warm. 'Go ahead then,' replies Sean. Big Mike walked right past, barely making eye contact. Sean made the left turn and as they were driving Leigh Anne was processing the whole situation and shook her head to herself in disbelief and tells Sean to turn around. He then turns the car around and heads in the direction of Big Mike. Leigh Anne calls out for him and Big Mike continues to walk. Leigh Anne demands the car to be stopped and runs after Michael.

She then confronts Michael and asks him why he was going to the gym. Big Mike remained quiet, still making no eye contact. She then repeats the question, 'Big Mike, why were you going to the gym?' And this time he replies with, 'because it's warm.' That's when her toned changed, her maternal and protective instincts kicked in. As she held back her emotions, she asked him if he had anywhere to stay and he nodded. She then said abruptly, 'Don't you dare lie to me.' Big Mike paused and then shook his head confirming that he had nowhere to stay.

Without hesitation she looks at him and says, 'come on then' and offers him a place to stay for the night. The movie is very moving and the character that Sandra plays is a character I absolutely adore. That scene was an example highlighting how Leigh Anne's empathy and social intelligence was able to keep a boy warm and eventually save his life.

The point here is that we all have the ability to connect with people at such a high level to the point where we feel them before we hear them. We read their body language, we become masters of how to help others deal with their events and setbacks. What about yourself? What is your level of self-awareness and are you able to connect with yourself?

Dr Daniel Goldman says, *'That emotional intelligence is the ability to identify, access and control one's own emotions, the emotions of others and that of groups.'* The point intended in this part of the chapter is to help you identify your own emotions and what they are trying to tell you, which may have seemed pointless until now. But think about it, how you can live a better life if you can't identify and move past scars? In order to be able to process and deal with any unpleasant life experiences, you need to allow yourself to shift your perception about yourself or that event. I say *allow yourself* to see that event in a different light, because when you're a victim of any circumstance you intuitively defend the title as being the victim to that event until you feel like some justice is served. That kind of attitude will only empower that event to have a hold on how you handle any other similar situation, which may have held you back on achieving something worthwhile in your life. Which is why I would encourage you to adopt a growth mindset attitude, one that would allow you to see that experience as an opportunity to grow. Whenever I found myself in a position where I felt like I was mistreated or felt like I failed, I would process the outcome by asking my subconscious one simple question, and that was, 'what lesson am I supposed to learn from this experience?' The end result saw me appreciate the lesson as a reminder to never allow myself to be exposed to that level of disappointment, rendering me to be empowered again. All it took was being able to identify and process the emotions I had experienced.

Another reason why this topic is so important is that there was a study by neuroscientists that suggests that when an emotion gets triggered that chemicals are now released by the brain into our bloodstreams, which then activate biological sensations that are relevant to the triggered emotion. What that shows is that what we feel is actually experienced first as a biological or physical sensation, and if those biological sensations become a regular experience then those emotions creating those experiences will become a default setting and the body will eventually look for those sensations to help it make sense of the day. It effectively becomes your emotional addiction and that rush the body gets become a fix that the body needs.

Before we can create your ideal outlook of the life you'd like to manifest, it's crucial you understand what it is that's holding you back and how on earth these programs became your default settings. Most importantly, why these emotions, addictions, habits and behaviours shape who you are and who you've become.

emotional addictions

How many times have you felt overwhelmed, anxious, tired, disjointed, emotional and then you said, 'I'm not sure why I'm feeling like this. Life is great, I have amazing support, a loving family, a stable job and great health.'

Emotional pain can become an addiction, when you're constantly exposed to feelings of anger and you're overwhelmed with feelings of sadness, guilt, depression or fear, the changes that happen in the brain will eventually produce a dependency on those feelings.

There is an abundance of scientific evidence that shows how addictive behaviours share the same neurological pathways of the reward centres of the brain, kind of like when a child has a tantrum at a shopping centre and so to keep them quiet you give them what they want or you give them a treat. Now the child associates that behaviour with a reward, even though the experience and action were negative. Equally, if the child gets an 'A' on an exam and you reward them with a gift that child will associate the 'A' with a reward.

As we have established, the emotions we feel are the product of an experience. How we process those emotions usually dictates how we act or react to that experience. The issue is that the longer we continue to react and allow that perception to control our day and our lives, the stronger the dependency to the feelings we will unconsciously create. When we become heightened the body releases a cascade of biochemical reactions, and if reactions persist for lengthy periods of time then that is referred to as an 'emotional refractory period', which is a fancy way of saying that the emotion has had a hold on you to the point it has shifted your perception and makes you focus on only the things that conforms with your current emotion and mood. For example, if the emotion you are experiencing is disappointment and a friend comes along and is excited with a potential opportunity you would quickly focus on the potential for that opportunity to fail and express that to your friend.

If you allow those same emotions to linger on they will eventually control your mood, your temperament and at some point you'll start to identify your life with those addictions; with pain and suffering it's because you're emotionally connected to it. That's when people will start saying things like, 'why are you so bitter or upset?' Your response is usually, 'because of this circumstance or because that person.' What you ultimately want to do is overcome all the emotions to any event that has kept you anchored to the past. Now just to clarify, I am in no way asking you to forget any events or disregard them; all I am saying is that if we can remove any associated emotions attached to the past traumatic event then the experience itself will render us some level of growth.

The way our brain is wired is that we only see what we believe is possible; we match patterns that exist within ourselves and our environment that ultimately recreates our own reality. Our emotions become the bridge between the mind and the body, they are very present and are what is dictating the choices we make, and those choices are 99% subconscious which is why your life is a blueprint of your subconscious behaviour.

When the body becomes dependent on any particular chemical response to our familiar emotions, it immediately triggers a cellular response; neurotransmitters are released and our physiology begins to shift to suit the trigger of that emotion. Over a period of time those reactions strengthen the neurological pathways until they become your new default program. That is when the body becomes dependent on that chemical rush that the neurotransmitters are getting and are perceived as a reward.

Emotions are a natural energy response to what we experience through our senses. They function as a guidance system for all our decisions and actions. Candace Pert shows in her research that all emotions are biochemical reactions that can either harm or heal the body. In the *Power of Now*, Eckhart Tolle said, 'Every addiction arises from an unconscious refusal to face and move through your own pain'. When we attempt to change, the cells yell out to your brain saying, 'hey, we haven't had our fix yet', and then start to send impressions to the brain relevant to the addiction. That's when your brain starts to scan the room, your environment or your past experiences and memories in search of anything that would help the brain find an impression that is appropriate to the chemical addiction.

The brain will continue to ruminate and scan through its archives of data until it finds an image or an experience to match the chemical reaction the body is craving. That's when the body says, 'Ah, this feels right.' You've now fulfilled the biochemical craving by creating it and finding a situation that met those biochemical needs.

Now you know why at times you feel uneasy and the easiest way to put it is that the brain and the body are not in coherence. If you haven't been able to control your emotional state and continually find yourself repeating the same behaviours and experiencing the same types of situations, then it may just be that you're addicted to your emotions.

how we encode emotions

Fear and anxiety live in an area of the brain known as the amygdala, which is located a couple of inches in from the ears. An interesting fact: all mammals have the same reflex experience as humans, because they're wired the same way. When we see an image that creates any type of fearful stimulus the sensory receptors and muscles in our eyes known as the 'Superior Colliculus' immediately activates the *thalamus*, which is also referred to as our relay system as its main job is to relay the *'motor and sensory'* signals to the cerebral cortex (our analytical and creative mind). This now activates our awareness to the fear of the visual image.

The really impressive thing is that milliseconds prior to the cerebral cortex being notified of the potentially life-threatening stimulus, the thalamus sent a signal to the amygdala notifying it of the potential threat to our environment, which now activates our subconscious hardwired program as a reflex to that stimulus. If a gunman walks into a bank, before the cashier gets a chance to analyse the situation and the safety of innocent people in the bank, the cashier presses the secret button signalling help to the police. Then the cashier complies in order to keep the gunman calm and stall time until the police arrive.

You can say that the protocol the cashier followed was all processed by the analytical mind and the security button pressed was exactly like the amygdala being notified and in turn activated your security plan.

Our brains are wired to look out for threats or pleasures and so as soon as either one is detected then a release of chemical messengers are activated. For example, the fear of seeing a snake will release our stress hormones adrenaline and cortisol to help prepare us for either a fight or flight response. Equally, if we experience something that is good, like your parents buying you your first car, then the biochemical response is a release of dopamine, oxytocin and serotonin, which are the chemicals that make us feel joyful and happy.

The reward centre responds to new information from the nervous system by releasing neurotransmitters, which are the *'biochemical messengers.'* Their job is to pass on a signal or message from one neuron to another or to a cell that it wants to activate. Our brains have over a hundred neurotransmitters, yet the ones that are linked to our addictions are the ones that are key to our survival or success. It's through this reward system that we've basically invented addiction and is why addictions are learnt behaviours and not restricted or limited to only narcotics. Our behaviours and things like sugary sweets are just as addictive because they all use the same brain circuitry.

The point is that in both positive or negative instances the feeling system is activated before the thinking system and so we feel the sensations to the emotions before we see them and as a result we become reactive instead of being responsive. We then revert back to the subconscious habits and usually don't think rationally. It's almost as though in the heat of the moment our emotions hijack our brains.

The final message is that our emotions play a major part in how we see the world, and most importantly, how we end up seeing our lives. If you can learn from the emotions through experiences you don't want and instead reframe them with the thoughts, feelings and experiences that you do want, then life begins to improve immediately.

If you're wondering how on earth you can do that, trust in your process and by the time you read the last page of this book it'll all just make sense. You may even learn that you actually have had all your answers already.

chapter 3:
BodyMind

So that you are able to better understand how it is that our thoughts, perceptions, beliefs and emotions can literally impact and change our genetic expression, I thought it would be best to drip feed the information, so that it's easier for you to digest and understand. Remember this is a journey of growth and reconnecting with yourself, so go at a pace that you feel comfortable with.

When I was studying Zen, the prevailing wisdom was to *challenge your unexamined beliefs, to no longer be imprisoned by your own ignorance,* and that freedom is found in self-awareness. Up until this point we've outlined how the brain controls the biochemistry of the blood, and that the fate of the biochemical reactions we experience is controlled by our emotions and thoughts. Now I want to introduce you to the idea that the fate of your cells are also at the mercy of those exact same bio-chemical influences. Our cells make up every part of our existence and science proves that our blood is heavily influenced by our biochemistry. Science also proves that our blood is an excellent source of our human DNA, and lastly science also proves that our DNA is largely found in the nucleus of a cell.

I've purposely called this chapter BodyMind without a hyphen or space because there is no isolated existence of one without the other. Here is where we start to add one of the most important pieces to this puzzle; that is how our thoughts, our emotions, our environment and our beliefs change our genetic expression.

Let's imagine you had a clone, an identical you, and that clone was taken away to a foreign place, but you were taken to a sophisticated home with classical music being played, private schools, piano and tennis instructors, and parents who taught you the importance of mindful meditation. Yet your clone in the foreign place was raised in an orphanage and was constantly shown disappointment and abandonment and so he developed his own survival tools and always looked for how he could make a quick buck or get the most out of an opportunity as life has been stressful and difficult.

Now if you are reunited at the age of 30, chances are you would look and act differently. I was referring to the movie *Twins* as my example, starring Arnold Schwarzenegger and Danny DeVito. They were part of a genetic experiment and were separated at birth. Julius, who is played by Arnold, was raised by a scientist and grows up humble, intelligent and strong, but very naive about the larger world. On the other hand, Vincent, who is played by Danny DeVito, grows up to be an unscrupulous street hustler, struggling to make a living in Los Angeles. Now if scientists were to look at their genetic code they would say that their DNA was exactly the same as each other. The new science known as 'Epigenetics' is the science that shows it's possible.

Here's the way it works, at the risk of sounding too 'science-y', every cell is controlled by either a methyl group or a histone, which are groups of proteins. Every cell has a distinct methylation and histone pattern and that's what effectively gives the cells its designated role in the body. For example, a skin cell or a hair cell. The DNA is like a computer and the methyl and histone are the software that play an important role in gene regulation; the way genes are put together.

The makeup of your DNA will stay the same throughout your entire life, but it's these proteins that help select the genes that either get expressed or that don't. The make-up of chemical compounds and proteins that can attach to DNA is referred to as the 'Epigenome'. This can, and will change throughout your life to suit your circumstance or environment. If it sounds a little confusing at this present moment, don't worry, because it'll all start to make sense and you'll get to untangle this puzzle and finally understand that what we do, how we think, what we eat, what we believe and what we perceive affects our genetic expression and that our cells are a technology that turns an experience into biology.

perception and your brain

Perception is our ability to understand the meaning that is picked up by our senses in order to better interpret and experience the world. However, there are times that what you perceive isn't what you think you see. At an early age we're taught about our five senses: sight, hearing, taste, touch and smell, and how important they are to experience the world and stimuli around us. For example vision, your ability to see an image, is the result of a very impressive series of events. Light bounces off an object and into your eyes, your eyes take in all of the varied energy, which now gets transferred into neural messages. The brain now processes these messages and organises them into the image you see.

Our senses wouldn't mean a thing to us without our brain's ability to translate the sensory information into our perception. For example, without the ability to interpret a scent, we wouldn't be able to determine the difference between the smell of garbage or our favourite fragrance.

The downside to this is that our brains can easily be tricked because we generate our perception on a world that's useful for us to see. This world has been shaped by our beliefs, and in our minds our beliefs are true and final, and so we now live out our lives based on a belief and a perception of a life that could be creating the setbacks that we're continuing to experience.

Let's look at motion as an example, two balls moving at the same speed, one large and one small. Our brains perceive the larger ball to be moving slower than the smaller ball, but in actual fact they're both moving at the same pace. It's illusions like this that prove to us that we don't see the world as it is, but rather we see the world as we are; it's actually our perceptions that are limited, as they can only reflect what they know to be true. Therefore, we create what we're expecting and what we see is what we expect to see. That's simply because we can't see the things we've never seen before. You don't know what to look for!

There is a South Asian parable known as *'The Blind Men and an Elephant'* where there was a group of six blind men that were given the opportunity to experience an elephant and then asked to describe what they thought an elephant is. Each of these men were confined to an area of the elephant. For example, the tail, or the leg or the tusks. The blind man touching the tail said, 'I know what an elephant is, it's like rope.' The man touching the legs said, 'No, an elephant is a pillar, like a tree trunk.' The blind man touching the tusk said, 'An elephant is smooth and hard like a spear.' And so on, until the elephant was described in six different ways. The significance of this parable is that individually there was no way that any one of these blind men could fully appreciate the elephant because of their limited perspective.

The point is that we all have our own take on reality that may not be the complete picture, much like the men in the parable, and that's because we're born into a culture and ideals that precedes us. We then take these cultural ideals and narratives and allow them to define us and shape who we become by spinning out our own set of ideals, and so as a consequence our lives become reflective of our perceptual beliefs, ideals, habits and experiences.

If at any time you feel like there might be a chance that there is a gap between your perception and your reality, then I would suggest you get yourself a notebook and make notes and as you develop a better understanding throughout your journey then you can reflect and close that gap by using all this new found wisdom and instead install the new programs that will allow you to finally see the world that you've always desired and an environment that has become an extension of your dreams and aspirations.

||||||||||||||||||||||||||||||||||||||||||||||||||||||

No longer limit yourself to the beliefs of your past habits and experiences.

||||||||||||||||||||||||||||||||||||||||||||||||||||||

bio-electric cells

Cells: Out with the Old, in with the New

Some of the biggest scientific and spiritual debates that have taken place have been about what it is that determines our future. Is it our genetics? Is it evolution? Or is it our environment? A question to get you thinking and if you can take a moment to process it before reading on. Is your life, your future predetermined? Or do you actually get to have a say in creating your future?

The picture that should be emerging is that you're not necessarily the victim of your genes as you may have once perceived and that your life isn't out of your control; and that your thoughts, your beliefs and behaviours have ultimately been controlling the life that you have been experiencing to this date. Conventional belief is that at the moment of fertilisation you receive a set of genes from your mother and a set from your father. Those two sets come together and the result of those genes become your fate in life as an individual. Traditional science has taught us that we didn't pick our genes. It would be right, we didn't. It has also convinced us that we cannot change our genes and that these genes ultimately govern our fate and control our biology. In short, this old understanding is one that depicts that we can't control our fate, rendering this model one that has become a liability to how we live out our lives. The new understanding is that we genuinely aren't victims, and that we're not limited to those past beliefs, but rather that we are creators, and that we can manifest and attract whatever it is that we desire in life.

In the medical world, the 'human biology' is treated as though it's this machine that is full of biochemicals and that it is controlled by its genes; so when you visit your doctor, the belief system of the doctor is that the problem has to be either in the makeup of your genes or biochemistry and that there can be no other explanation. They punch all your symptoms and data into a computer, which then tells the doctor what medication they should be prescribing. In some sense this belief system renders people to feel powerless over their own life, because apparently they didn't pick their genes and they can't change their genes. They believe that those same genes control who they are, and so naturally people will start to feel like victims, as they have absolutely no control over the outcomes and experiences of their lives. As a consequence, we've seen the development of a race assuming less accountability for their health and wellbeing who have adopted the mindset of, 'If we can't change, then why should we care', as a valid reason and excuse to neglect themselves. Conventional science to this day still continues to suggest that we're victims and that our lives are predetermined and that we just have to make the most of what we can and what we have to work with. Priming people into a severe state of fear, which sees us taking all sorts of preventative medicines making the pharmaceutical company's pockets grow fatter.

Quantum physics and the *'Human Genome Project'* have helped with this understanding as they provided medical and scientific breakthroughs by providing substantial evidence that 'our genes' do not necessarily control life. This has given us a brand-new way of thinking and understanding of our biology. These fields have shown that we actually have total agency in controlling or affecting the way our cells function. Scientific research of genetic modification and altering the makeup of the genes can be seen as an attempt to create a superhuman, and these studies provide more scientific evidence highlighting how those manipulations can influence human behaviour and emotions. The genes now begin to take on a more profound meaning on our biology and the ultimate finding is that these genes actually influence the character and traits of the human and not just their physical appearance.

Genes are only a blueprint in one's life and not the architect. When we experience emotional states of anger, guilt, excitement or happiness, each of those individual emotions release an outbreak of neuropeptides that are unique to that emotional state. Where it all gets interesting is that when cells split and clone themselves, the new cell takes on the same beliefs and it starts to allow more receptors in the new cell to match that specific peptide to those same recurring and habitual emotions. So if you're constantly living through the perceptual lens and beliefs that you're the victim, then you are programming your cells. Actually, you're giving them the approval to increase the receptors relevant to those negative emotions, as a consequence you're now lessening the number of positive receptor sites as there's a limit to how many receptor sites are on each cell.

The state of our Body and Mind (our 'BodyMind') and the influencing factors of our genes and DNA, is a direct reflection of our environment, our thoughts and beliefs, which in turn activates or inhibits the expression of our genes. The new science epigenetics confirms and validates that that's exactly the case, 'Epi' meaning outside our genetics. Here is an oversimplified explanation of how this works, the epigenetic effects on your cells happen as your cells start to divide, that's when they start receiving signals and information from surrounding cells, kind of like when you go to a new school and then you meet a group of new friends and they start to warn you about the class you're taking, certain people and certain teachers. Now you know who to avoid and how to please the teacher. That's the same with our cells; it's because of the new information the relevant genes begin to get turned on whilst others get turned off.

Epigenetics has effectively taught us how our genes express themselves and has proved that your genes are a product of your experiences, beliefs and environment. As soon as you begin to introduce beliefs and the emotions to what you wish to manifest, then the environment you wish to experience would eventually become a consequence of those positive changes. This makes you the creator of your own life and happiness. Remember, your cells are a technology that turn experience into biology. They must, because your main goal is to stay alive and so your cells will absorb the information of your thoughts, beliefs and the biochemical cascade that your emotions trigger. That information will be relayed so that the body now adjusts to your experience or reinforces whatever your belief system is. Your mind and body are one big kinetic chain and so your body will put into action and streamline you to be efficient, by helping you unconsciously integrate all the biological responses to suit your beliefs.

placebo and nocebo paradox

This is the paradox of how the mind can heal the body. It's called the placebo effect, a medical term that basically means, an inert substance with no inherent pharmacological activity; meaning a substance that has no therapeutic effect. When a test is conducted on any medication, the test subjects are divided into two groups, one group would actually be taking the medication and the other would take nothing more than a sugar pill. This is referred to as the *'double blind test'* and all test subjects would be under the impression that they would be getting the medication and the result in most cases was that the subjects taking the sugar pill would also heal from the disease or illness being tested.

There is a database known as 'The Spontaneous Remission Project' that has over 3,500 cases of patients who have miraculously healed from apparently incurable illnesses. This scientific phenomena is evidence that we have this innate self-repair mechanism that can help more than pharmaceuticals in some cases.

Placebo in Latin means 'I will please' or 'I will satisfy'. The medical term was first used in the 1700s to describe something that was given to make the patient happy rather than to help them. But the placebo isn't just in the mind, it's in our physiology; it's actually measurable and so in an attempt to further understand, other placebo tests were implemented and then studied. For example, in what is referred to as a *'Sham Surgical Placebo'*, test subjects were given general anaesthetic and then a superficial procedure was performed. A small skin incision was made without the actual surgery being performed. The finding was that the patient would also sometimes miraculously heal from the illness or disease.

The interesting thing is that in this scientific research they found that they could improve how effective the test subjects were able to heal by improving the environment that was surrounding the pill or procedure. For example the emotional support or empathy the test subject received, which now highlighted that it wasn't just the belief in the pill that allowed them to heal, it was also the environment surrounding that pill that could affect the outcome. Again the most important point to take from this is that the environment that surrounds the cells also determines the outcome of how that cell behaves, whether it be pills or perception.

An example of how productive the placebo effect is, there was a study that was carried out on the effectiveness of an antidepressant in respects to depression, which resulted that over 80 percent of the test subjects that were given the innate placebo sugar pill healed as well as the test subjects who were actually taking the medication. I find it fascinating that the subjects who believed they were getting the medication or treatment and only received a sugar pill were able to somehow replicate the effect of the medication they thought they were taking. It could be that this inert placebo activated the body's innate ability to heal itself by just a thought or a belief.

The power of positive thoughts has been shown that it can heal an individual, but what about negative thoughts or beliefs? Could they be equally as effective in creating an illness or the belief in the effects of the illness? It's possible and it's referred to as the 'Nocebo effect' translated as 'I will harm' in Latin.

In a study of fibromyalgia, 10 percent of the subjects who were taking the inert sugar pill dropped out because they were experiencing the symptoms of the side effects. In particular, the nausea that they were warned about. Tell me you don't find that fascinating that they were able to manifest the exact side effect they were told even though they were merely taking a sugar pill? In further studies of the nocebo effect, the patients who were taking real medication that read the list of side effects found that they were experiencing the side effects that were listed. Yet on the flip side of that test the subjects that weren't aware of the side effects felt no side effects, none! The obvious point here is that both negative thinking or negative beliefs can just as easily cause a disease or its symptom to manifest, just as easily as positive thoughts and positive beliefs have the ability to heal the body from a disease.

From an evolutionary standpoint this innate paradox makes complete sense simply because when we were created, we weren't created as Adam, Eve, a doctor and a compounding pharmacist. Instead, we were created with this incredible gift and that is the ability to heal ourselves. However, as time has gone on and through technological breakthroughs and the inception of limiting beliefs we have lost the ability to listen to ourselves. As a result we find ourselves continually looking for something outside ourselves to make us look and feel better.

IIIIIIIIIIIIIIIIIIIIIIIIIIIIIIIIIIIIIIIIIIIIIIIIIIIIII

'Be Enthusiastic-
Remember the Placebo Effect,
30% of medicine is show business.'
~ Ronald Spark

IIIIIIIIIIIIIIIIIIIIIIIIIIIIIIIIIIIIIIIIIIIIIIIIIIIIII

the mind that heals the body

The last point I would like to make before we move onto the next topic is that cells are significant as all of life is made up of cells. Yet I feel like their significance is so overlooked even though there is more technology in one cell of the body than there is in a Formula 1 Racing Car. The makeup of our bodies is trillions of cells and the coolest thing is that there is absolutely no new function in your entire body that isn't already present in every cell. Every cell has a respiratory system, a digestive system, an endocrine system, a reproductive system, a nervous system, even an immune system. We now know the significance of positive thinking and how positive emotions can affect us at a cellular level, we've also discussed how positive thoughts and positive emotions can create profound improvements to one's life or just as easily negative thoughts and emotions can destroy one's life. We have also outlined how emotions were incredibly important for our survival and how we eventually were able to place labels on those emotions, we then addressed how powerful the mind is in creating biological changes.

When we have an emotionally charged experience, memory or belief, that experience activates the brain's limbic system, where it gets processed and a chain-reaction release of the relevant biochemicals equal to that thought, belief and perception. The point is that these biochemicals need to find a place that is made for them and so they head directly for their targeted receptors.

Candice Pert, who is a molecular biologist and psycho-neuro-immunologist (which is a fancy word for the study of the effect of the mind on health and resistance to disease) explains in her book *Molecules of Emotions* that the way emotions and receptors typically unite is likened to a key fitting into a lock, and so that there alone is enough proof that if your body has the receptor for the pharmaceutical you've been prescribed, then the receptor is indication that you have the ability to produce that exact pharmaceutical yourself; but your BodyMind can only produce what you believe to be true. This may take some time for you to get your head around, I respect that. My intention is to merely give you the facts and allow you to explore the rest yourself through applying any information you find useful to use.

I sincerely pray that you realise the impacts that negative emotions, thoughts and beliefs have on the outcome of your health, your well-being and life; and that you will think twice before allowing the toxic cycle of negative thinking to continue to manifest and control you. I would bet my life on the fact that if someone spoke to you the way you speak to yourself, you would stop speaking to them or confront them. Why is it that you allow yourself to do so? If that is something you are guilty of, it's now time to change. Especially when you now know that your cells absorb everything you say, believe and feel. I have to admit, delivering the content of this chapter in a way where it did not overwhelm you with six syllable words but was still enough to showcase how profound the topics were in creating sustainable change, was a little challenging. There were so many components that go into understanding how it is you that your body, mind and emotions all go into improving your life, your health, and wellbeing.

Lastly, the way our brain is wired is that we only see what we believe is possible; we match patterns that already exist within ourselves, which then creates our own reality. Our emotions bridge between the mind and body, they are very present and are what keeps us alive and helps us make choices every single moment of the day. Remember that your perception and your environment controls your cells, and that at a cellular level your perceptions are just perceptions; but at the human levels perceptions are beliefs and our beliefs affect our cells, they select our genes, select our behaviour and ultimately shape the outcome of our life, health, and wellbeing. Knowing this, can now be *life changing*.

||||||||||||||||||||||||||||||||||||||||||||||||||||||||

'Everything is energy
and that's all there is to it.
Match the frequency of the reality
you want and you cannot help
but get that reality.
There can be no other way.
This is not philosophy.
This is physics.'
~ Albert Einstein

||||||||||||||||||||||||||||||||||||||||||||||||||||||||

chapter 4:
energy

The significance of energy and why it is that we keep attracting the same things in our lives.

How many times have we heard or seen this, your best friend breaks up with her boyfriend, your friend relies heavily on the support of yourself and her closest friends, you all get together regularly for D&Ms, weekly movie nights with some wine and chocolates, a few months pass by and she's now ready to start dating. But somehow she attracts the same kind of guy, and experiences the same types of experiences all over again, why is that?

It's not a matter of having bad luck with guys, there is no lucky dip of whether you find the perfect partner or a toxic one. It's basically what you allow in your field and what you allow yourself to continue to be exposed to. Your experiences, beliefs and thoughts are all energy and *'like energy will only attract the same kind of energy'*.

Nicola Tesla famously said, *'To find the secrets of the universe, think in terms of energy, frequency and vibration. Everything is energy that vibrates at a certain frequency.'*

Traditional science teaches us that atoms are tiny particles of matter and the defining structure of elements. However, in the early 1900s physicists studied these particles as they wanted to know what they were made out of. Through extensive research the new finding was that there were even smaller particles within them, which were later named electrons, protons and neutrons. This new discovery sparked more interest in exploring these newfound smaller particles and effectively the world changed, because the ultimate finding by quantum physicists is that atoms, protons, electrons and neutrons are not made out of anything physical, they're made out of energy. We are one big energy field and wherever we go we're like a broadcast; we vibrate and broadcast energy to everything, much like a radio. If that frequency resonates with anything then that energy can either positively or negatively influence and affect whatever it is resonating with.

Why does this matter? It matters because your life is a manifestation of where you direct your energy, for example, if you watered the garden, would the weeds grow or the flowers grow? Both! Because water does not discriminate between the weeds or the flowers, and that's the same with energy. If you invest your energy into anything negative then, just like weeds it will grow into something more negative. Equally, if you invest your energy in something positive, that will also grow and become more positive. Energy is a communication that has nothing to do with words, it is always available and if you want to feel it then all you need to do is become aware of it, by the time you reach the end of the book you will have a newfound appreciation for it. And learn that your life is a sum total of where you invest your energy.

The issue with most people these days is that we neglect to listen to what energy, or our intuition is trying to tell us. For example, 'Am I with people who support me?' Or 'is this the right job for me?' We dismiss all the intuitive feedback we get from our intuition and environment; we've lost faith in that innate feedback system we were gifted with. Instead we've become so fixated on the fact it must be present to be real and that is the kind of mentality that gives rise for you to have the excuse of, 'I will change when my environment changes', giving you the warped sense of self-justification on why your life hasn't changed. The loss of belief is a sad way to live.

The amazing thing about belief is that when you can have the feeling and the belief as though you have whatever it is you desire then who cares whether you have it or not? I mean think about it, you already feel as though you have it. This is something that will begin to explain itself as you continue to read on. Your *intuition* is like a muscle and the more you exercise it, the stronger the bond between you and the information your intuition is expressing to you will become. However, the more you dismiss the feedback you get then the greater the wedge you drive between you and this innate gift you were created with, e.g., when you intuitively get the 'this doesn't feel right to me' feeling and then you dismiss it by saying 'I'm just being paranoid, I'm always overthinking things'. That has been the driving force between your behaviour and your environment, by that I mean that we only believe to be true what we see in our environment causing us to ultimately be controlled by what we see and hear instead of feel.

Can you imagine how your life would be if you learnt how to manage your energy? We all have a certain amount of energy, yet daily we continue to invest our energy into people and things around us that don't appreciate it, until we have no energy left. Your energy is the most precious asset you have in life, even more valuable than money. It may be about time you started treating your energy the same way an investment banker treats money because energy, like money, is also a resource that needs to be invested and managed wisely. Here's why: everything is made up of energy that vibrates at a certain frequency, and you honestly cannot move forward in life to the places you desire to be at with energy that brings you down and sucks the life-force from you.

The message here is that you're not only responsible for the energy you bring into your life, but you're also responsible for the energy you surround yourself with. Which means you may need to recognise and take responsibility for the energy that you allow to be brought into your space by doing a clearing of the people whose energy is not supportive of who you desire to be in life. Once you do, you will immediately feel like a burden has been lifted and is when you will start to see that there is so much more to you than you perceive. In all beings or things there is a level of consciousness and that carries its own frequency, energy and vibration and the amazing thing about it all is that all of it is connected.

the thoughts create vibration and frequency

Here is the deal with thoughts. Science tells us that all matter is made up of atoms and we've just established that atoms are energy. So if the brain is made up of grey matter and atoms are what the matter is composed of then it would be fair to say that our brains would be made up of energy. Equally, if our circling world as we know it, is also composed of the same incredible atoms and matter, then it would make perfect sense that this mighty power also attracts the things that resonate with our thoughts as well as our desires and fears.

In order to better understand how thoughts change your energy, frequency and vibration and in return how they attract the same of what you continue to believe and feel, we must first understand and appreciate what atoms and matter really are.

Matter is basically any object that occupies space, whether it be in the form of a gas, liquid or a solid, each one of these forms are made up of millions of tiny particles called atoms. 'Atom' comes from the Greek word *Atomos* which means *indivisible* and the best way to describe the structure or make up of an atom is likened to a hardboiled egg that's cut in half; the egg yolk is the yellow bit in the centre and the egg white encapsulates it. The amount of egg whites to an egg is relevant to the size or the weight of the egg.

That's exactly like an atom, the nucleus is like the yolk and that's made up of protons and neutrons and orbiting the nucleus are electrons, much like how the egg white surrounds the egg yolk. The size or the weight of the atom depends on how many electrons are orbiting the nucleus.

Atoms are the building blocks of matter that quite literally make up our entire universe. Isn't it amazing that everything in our life and the world as we know it is made up of atoms? Here is where how these atoms are constructed and how they create their frequency gets interesting. Electrons orbit the nucleus in a designated sphere and the amazing thing is that they never collide. That just blows me away to be honest. Even though these electrons never collide, what they do cause is friction. This happens as the orbiting electrons pass each other which now creates a wave, those waves make up a certain frequency; kind of like when you drop a pebble in a lake that's still, it causes a ripple effect and so frequency is ultimately the distance between the wavelengths or ripples in that lake.

The frequency at which the electron vibrates at is directly proportional to the total energy of that electron; and the higher the energy atomic state of the electron then the quicker the vibrational frequency will be. In short, electrons are a quantum object with wave-like properties that must always be vibrating at some frequency. Being that the brain is made up of electrons, every time you shift your thoughts onto something or someone you end up changing the rate of vibration, so the movement or displacement of these electrons through your thoughts, beliefs and emotions create the frequencies that impact both your energy and your biochemistry either positively or negatively.

Even something as simple as having a general everyday conversation with someone can cause the brains to work 'in sync' and that's because the rhythms of brainwaves between the two people taking part in the conversation begin to match each other and eventually become coherent. If ever you've experienced this when it happens you may have started to feel a little weird and maybe even mentioned it to the person you were having a conversation with. As you both began to understand each other's feelings, ideas, beliefs you may even start to finish off each other's sentences and start sharing reciprocal behaviours, such as posture mirroring, or find an increased coordination in your verbal and nonverbal interactions with each other. Another example of coherence is with women that spend a lot of time together and end up sharing menstrual synchrony when having their period or menstrual cycles.

the power of words and thoughts

|||||||||||||||||||||||||||||||||||||||||||||||||||||||

'It is the mark of an educated mind to be able to entertain a thought without accepting it.'
~ Aristotle

|||||||||||||||||||||||||||||||||||||||||||||||||||||||

The intention is to show you that you are honestly capable of so much more than you know. In order to see that, you must choose the right words and have the right thoughts. Words are powerful, using the right words can inspire a nation or in this case change your life. There has been so much hype about the power of positive thinking, the question is does it work?

Remember when you were a child when you'd say, sticks and stones will break my bones but words will never hurt me? Well that might have been a lie because words do hurt, they do matter. Words can either attack or they can attract. Words can shape your future because they ultimately become things. For example, when you say to yourself, 'this is too good to be true, something is bound to happen.' And sure enough something does end up happening. Does this sound familiar? Rumi is one of my favourite poets and theologians and he famously quoted that *'We carry inside us, the wonders we seek outside us.'* Take the time to process that, because that ultimately implies that we are the creators of whatever it is that we desire. Every moment, every choice is rendering who we become in the next moment, kind of like when you're watching a movie online and it starts buffering the next few percent, every time you make a choice it's literally buffering the next moment. So our choices do matter and there are real consequences to our actions, for what we choose, we become. We've just outlined how the new science of epigenetics is proving that we can turn experience into biology, that our experiences are written all over our bodies, that our choice of words governs our fate, which proves that we have total control of creating our future self. You may be asking, why does this matter? It matters because we all want our lives to stand for something, to have meaning. It matters because we have the opportunity to do something meaningful with our lives, it matters because life exists inside these individual moments and it's up to us to make the most of them.

The language we use helps us to express our thoughts, the choice of words help us to compose our thoughts and they also help us change our thoughts as words are a means of interacting with our environment. The problem is that most of us are so reactive that we allow our environment to control how we think, act and feel. If we want to start feeling better we need to start focussing on what it is that we're thinking about. Because as we've established, it's our thoughts that create our feelings and our feelings dictate our behaviours because our thoughts become things, our thoughts help form the language we use in our conversations, our words now become what we focus on and ultimately fuels our behaviour, and our behaviours become an action.

Positive thinking helps improve performance, relationships and even one's career because when you think better about yourself and the world around you the natural outcome is that you end up interacting with your world in a way that allows you to become the creator of the environment you desire. There was this study that was conducted on what the variables were between the top five tennis superstars compared to their competition peers and the ultimate finding was that it was their thought process and choice of words that was the catalyst in creating the gap between them and the rest of the playing field. It wasn't their nutrition or their training program, it was how they thought and what they said to themselves. For example, when they would lose a point they wouldn't yell and carry on, they would compose themselves, acknowledge their mishap and that their opponent played a great shot by saying things like, 'that was a nice shot, but I dare you to try that again' or 'I will win that point back' and embrace the challenge. By doing this they were able to slow down their heart rate, which helped slow down their breathing rate, which ultimately resulted in conserving energy and over the space of the game and tournament that alone was the edge they needed.

Words are like seeds. When you speak something out, you're now giving it life and what you plant will inevitably be the fruit you end up harvesting. I mean you can't keep planting negative thoughts and expect a positive outcome. Equally you can't continue to talk about your debts and expect abundance to manifest, my advice is that you stop using words to describe your situation, but rather use the words that'll change it. And don't be disheartened by your negative thoughts because they come to us all; the key is not to indulge in a conversation with your thoughts. You can acknowledge them, but then tell them that those thoughts are no longer needed and that you're back in control. Thank them and go on about your day.

We have all had negative things happen to us or someone that has done us wrong. It's easy to go through life being offended, it's easy to live in self-pity and blaming others for the outcomes in your life. Truth is you're now giving that person or thing too much power and the more life you give it, then the longer it will keep you anchored in the past, reliving those same familiar emotions. All this does is leave you carrying this unnecessary baggage that will weigh you down and suck the life force from you.

The ultimate message here is that we all experience some form of pain, so don't just go through it, grow through it.

habitual vocabulary

**'Change your Words
to change your World'**

||||||||||||||||||||||||||||||||||||||||||||||||||||||||||

'A powerful agent is the right word.
Whenever we come upon one of
those intensely right words in a book
or a newspaper the resulting effect
is physical as well as spiritual,
and electrically prompt.'
~ Mark Twain

||||||||||||||||||||||||||||||||||||||||||||||||||||||||||

Is it possible that the words we attach to our experiences actually become our experience? Do words have any biochemical effects? Language shapes our behaviour and how we interact with our environment; the right words spoken in the right way can bring us love, money, respect and most importantly those words can move us away from the life we don't want. So the final message here is that we must carefully choose our words in order to create the right thoughts that correlate with our aspirations and whatever it is we view as our perfect life.

The world's greatest leaders and visionaries used the power of words to help to inspire others towards their vision and creating change. Martin Luther King's 'I have a dream' speech exposed the American public to the injustice of racial inequality and persuaded them to stop any discrimination on the basis of race. By masterfully using *Ethos* (values), *Pathos* (e-motions) and finally *Logos* (logic) he was able to inspire the nation into action; his words imprinted an image of what African Americans had been fighting to attain for over a hundred years, especially after Abraham Lincoln freed the slaves and the promises that were made to African Americans were not met. He brilliantly used certain analogies of Abraham Lincoln's emancipation proclamation speech, which enabled him to instantly connect with the millions of viewers who were watching his speech on TV, and the 200,000 plus people that were present at the Lincoln Memorial. By doing so he was able to frame the civil rights movement in a way that helped the audience grasp the structure and remember the nuance of his message so much so that 50 years later people are still talking about that speech.

Can changing your words really change your life? Can the words you use really ignite change, inspire action and improve your quality of life? It's evident that words shape our entire existence. Our words are a vehicle for expressing and sharing our experiences with others. More importantly, how we speak to ourselves directly influences how we experience things in life. If our internal self-talk is negative, chances are that our external experiences will also be negative.

Our brains are wired to work at high speeds, process information and constantly figure out ways to become more efficient. As a result, we resort to using the same words and thoughts over and over again. In the pursuit of efficiency, we often create the wrong kind of shortcuts. The problem is the words we choose unconsciously become our part of what is referred to as our habitual vocabulary. The same goes with our thoughts. We have approximately 70,000 thoughts circling in our minds and an astonishing 90 percent of them are the same habitual thoughts on repeat. So we tend to find ourselves starting the day 'awfulising' and catastrophising. When we experience distressing emotions, we unconsciously return to the default settings of our habitual vocabulary and our habitual thoughts. The thoughts and words that we attach to our experiences literally become our experience, equally as important, the words you choose and how you choose to say them will have a biochemical effect on the body, for example the minute you use a word like 'I'm shattered,' you're going to produce a very different biochemical effect than if you say, 'I'm a little disappointed.' Or if someone said to you, 'I think you're mistaken,' versus, 'I think you're wrong,' you would also have a different biochemical response. It's the exact same process that happens with the words that we use and say to ourselves, yet we're less conscious of their impacts. The message here is that by simply implementing an intentional shift in the choice of words you now habitually use to describe your emotions and perceptions; you will inevitably change how you feel and improve the quality of your life. It's as simple as that.

I read that Confucius said, 'An inconvenience is an unrecognised opportunity.' Allow me to give you your first inconvenience and ask you to simply replace one word or phrase that will reframe the way you experience your day and any obstacles you may encounter; you must however keep repeating to yourself all day. For example, 'I am the happiest I have ever been. I'm as beautiful as I can be and it reflects in how I see my world.' Or my favourite one I use is, 'I allow many gifts and abundances to flow to me daily, I feel blessed every day, I am completely happy, my life is great and I enjoy all the great experiences that come to me now.' My suggestion is that when you say them smile and add the emotion and the belief that nothing can deter you from being anything but the happiest you've ever been. Simply try it out for a week and see how different you start to see yourself and how you deal with your day.

Shifting your emotional patterns is crucial in shaping your decisions, actions and life for the better. The idea is now you create a choice instead of a habitual reaction. Which will give you the power to change your experiences in life by lowering the intensity of any negative emotions to the point where they no longer control you. How extraordinary will your life be when you consistently lower the intensity of negative emotions and intensify the positive ones?

Start small, note the negative words you use on a consistent basis and ask yourself how you can change them. Can you be 'irritated' instead of 'devastated?' On the other hand, can you feel 'ecstatic' instead of 'pleased?' Your internal dialogue can and will change your life. Start creating beneficial habits today, and you'll quickly reach a more positive, joyful state. That's when you'll be able to go out and face the world with 'this is who I am, as unique as I am, take me as I am'. Once your new ideal has been incepted into the brain it's almost impossible to eradicate, because an idea that's fully formed and understood can transform the world. What you picture when you speak and how you react to the words you use will create the transformation you want.

chapter 5:
the human brain

Throughout our existence knowledge has proven to be the precursor to creating an experience. Here is where a general understanding of how the brain functions becomes imperative in understanding how to create sustainable change. What I have always found to have the most profound impact in changing a person's perception is by inspiring change through knowledge and choice, by educating them on the 'whats' and 'whys'. That knowledge now gives them a mental blueprint on how to achieve their ultimate purpose.

Here is an interesting scientific fact: did you know that any process that helps you change your perception, will also change the activity of the brain and the way the brain commands the mind to work? Hidden in that sentence is the fact that the *'mind'* is effectively the *'brain'* in action, it is the actioning of all the programs. The point here is that when you can change the way the brain works you're effectively changing your mind.

The mind takes its commands from the brain and then an action is performed that correlates with the request of the brain. The brain's job is to take in all of this sensory information that you're experiencing and work out what needs to be done in order to keep you in a state of equilibrium (balance). When people try and change they unconsciously react like addicts and that's because they have become addicted to their familiar emotional states of being. As the past thoughts, experiences and memories trigger the same behaviours over and over again, it eventually allows the body to have a dependency and become addicted to the trail of biochemistry that they leave, to the point that the body now literally begins to behave as though it has a mind of its own and as a consequence it continues to search for its next fix. This is why we find it hard to change and is also why we tend to have uncontrollable urges or do things like sabotage a positive situation and then think, 'why on earth did I just do that?' In this chapter we will address how we consciously create these programs and habits until they end up becoming our default subconscious program. More importantly we get to address why it is we keep manifesting the same experiences no matter how many times we try and change? Or why is it that when we try and use our conscious mind to change our subconscious programs to get out of a negative emotional state that we begin to feel like we're out of control? It quite simply comes down to the fact that the mind and the body are now incoherent as they are in opposite states of mind.

The brain mediates our perceptions, every emotion, every thought, every sensation that we have has a corresponding action in the brain. Our brains account for about 20% of our body's blood, oxygen and energy usage. This impressive organ houses approximately 100 billion neurons which make up to 10,000 synapses or synaptic connections, which are basically connections to other neurons. Now why does this information matter? It matters because these synaptic connections form the programs that effectively become your default habits and behaviours. Every thought, every action and every memory is stored and managed in those neural pathways. Our brain is multifunctional as different parts of the brain have different jobs and the most impressive thing, is that our intelligence, our beliefs and our behaviours are not fixed, that's because the brain is plastic. Now I don't mean that literally, but the scientific term neuroplasticity refers to the fact that the brain can actually change shape and continues to do so throughout your life. Our experiences end up rewiring our brains and minds and is why when we change the way our brain operates; we are literally changing our minds. The last point I'll make before we move onto the next topic is that every human brain seems to be different. I don't mean that in a trivial way, but rather in a meaningful way that ends up impacting our intellect, our growth and the kind of experiences we have. The brain has a remarkable capacity for storing information that is virtually infinite however its flaw is that it's also coupled with a highly fallible retrieval process.

experiencing vs. remembering

We're the most advanced and intelligent creatures on Earth, yet one of the biggest flaws is our inability to accurately remember the things that happen to us. For all of the beautiful and conversely terrifying experiences we capture them through the synapses in our brain, let's just refer to them as *'the snapshots that form our lives'*. We depend on our memories to inform us on anything we need to make a decision on, the point here is that they may not have been as reliable as you thought. Throughout this entire book we've highlighted how our *memories* can effectively keep us anchored in the past, and that these memories tend to govern our perceptions, beliefs, actions and experiences. It makes perfect sense to now explore how it is that we remember vs what we really actually experience. What you'll find is that it's highly possible that your past memories may not be what you entirely remember.

So many people fail at changing their lives because they think the same thoughts, act the same way, carry the same beliefs and yet they expect something miraculous to change in their lives, I'm sorry it doesn't work that way! However, throughout this book you'll have every opportunity to work on that and create sustainable change that is easy, simple and maybe even fun; and so your aim is to now let go of those past thoughts and change the associated beliefs. The best way to improve your life is to change the way you think.

Dr Daniel Kahneman says that 'We approach the present experience with the anticipated memory', and by that he means that we approach the present already anticipating the memory that we choose to keep. He referenced it to the Instagram generation, and I thought that was the perfect analogy as we all can relate to this. Think about it for a moment, this concept is largely responsible for the success of Facebook and Instagram, and it's that you get to capture a moment, then edit that moment and then give that same moment an emotional aroma with your choice of filter that now alters the truth about that moment. You then save it and it's now anchored as an emotional moment in your life. In the future you then look back upon that memory with a distorted sense of that perceptual reality and that's much like the brain and how we experience versus how we remember. According to Kahneman, we have two selves: the experiencing self and the remembering self. The experiencing self knows only the present moment. The remembering self is a storyteller and it can dictate our actions when we think of the future as an anticipated memory.

Your memory is unreliable even though you think it isn't, and it will lead you astray even though you think it won't. Your life may have unfolded much differently than you remember it now. Every memory you have is somehow altered by your preconceptions, your expectations, your prejudices and stereotypes, we have the ability to alter and edit what we want to remember just like our trusted Instagram filters. All of the good times you look back on now might not have happened exactly as you thought they did. Many of the bad times may not have nearly been as terrible as you remember and is why we genuinely need to stop focussing on our past experiences and start creating the ones we genuinely want to keep in life, it all starts with an *Intent*, then *Desire*, and most importantly the *Belief* that you've already achieved it. When you can combine these three powerful tools the way you experience things and what you choose to remember will automatically change.

The reasoning for the emphasis on stories and memories is, that in the end that's all we keep from life. The stories we remember are the changes we encounter, the beginnings, the endings and all the significant moments we experienced in our lives. The catalyst to how we remember these stories is simply based on what we found to be important to us at that moment in time. All of the in-between is lost to time and the mundane experiences are swept away by the brain to make room for new and potentially interesting memories. Do you remember a moment in time where you were possibly on school holidays and you spent the weekend away with family and friends? It was one of the best weekends of your life, yet whenever you retell the story you can basically sum it all up in half an hour. It's much like a movie. Our memory chooses to highlight points that resonate with our states of belief, even though our memory has absolutely no limit to what it can hold, yet a two- or three-day event has been compressed into 30 minutes of point forms and highlights. This fact makes evolutionary sense, and that is we tend to remember the dangers and the rewards of life, we highlight and remember what's familiar rather than the whole story. This is why an unchanging environment tends to make our memory a blur.

||||||||||||||||||||||||||||||||||||||||||||||||||||||

'Try not to resist the changes
that come your way.
Instead let life live through you.
And do not worry that your life
is turning upside down.
How do you know that the side
you are used to is better
than the one to come?'
~ Rumi

||||||||||||||||||||||||||||||||||||||||||||||||||||||

understanding brain waves

You'll notice that I intentionally tend to not get too 'science-y' unless it's necessary and this is a time where I feel it's very necessary. Inside our brain is thought to be approximately 100 billion neurons and that makes up approximately 10,000 synapses or connections that effectively become our programs of habit. Having a general understanding of brain wave frequencies, how they can impact us and how to use this information will become significant in being able to create the changes needed to achieve the goals you set for yourself. Neurons communicate by sending a small electrical rush or pulse between any of the networks of neurons; so as we go through our day-to-day routines millions of these electrical pulses work in a rhythmic pattern that can be measured. Just imagine that your brain is buzzing with millions of electrical pulses being passed between each of the neurons. As those signals are being emitted from the network of cells in a synchronised firing pattern, they become a repeated cycle that is referred to as a brainwave.

Our brainwaves change according to what we're doing and feeling. When slower brain waves are dominant we can feel tired, slow, sluggish, or dreamy, the higher frequencies are dominant when we feel wired, or hyper-alert. The descriptions in this section are only very broad descriptions to give you a general understanding on how the brain works but more importantly what frequency you need to aim for in order to reprogram your subconscious and attain what you do want in life rather than what you don't. Through what is known as an electro-encephalogram (EEG), the activity of the brain in the form of electrical pulses are measured in cycles per second or Hertz, which basically means how many times the pulses fire per second. The lower the number of cycles per second the lower the brain activity. Equally, the higher the number of cycles per second the higher brain activity, these brain wave pattern cycles have been categorised into traditional groups.

The reason why this information is so important is that every one of our thoughts has a frequency and the ultimate finding is that these frequencies determine our states of mind. The function of your brain is to create meaning between your external world and your internal world and every time you shift your attention onto your external environment you begin to experience a certain level of awareness and in that moment your brain shifts into its relevant brain wave state to process any of the sensory information that comes in, so now you begin experiencing. Conversely if you calm your racing mind and shift your attention to your inner self then the activity of the brain will also slow down and your brain wave frequency will be relevant to your state of being which opens up the gates for a myriad of benefits, for example:

1. **Delta brainwaves**, when we are in delta we are also in what's recognised as our restorative sleep, the deep sleep where healing takes place because hormones such as prolactin and human growth hormone are released when your brain is in this state. When a baby is born, up until the age of two the baby's brain wave activity is said to be in *Delta* which explains why the newborn can't remain awake for more than a few hours at a time. The baby also operates predominantly from the subconscious mind and is effectively absorbing all the stimuli of his or her environment.

2. **Theta is our gateway to learning, memory, and intuition.** In theta, our senses are withdrawn from our external environment and focussed on the signals originating from within us. It's almost like a

twilight state which we normally only experience for a very brief time as we wake or drift off to sleep. In theta we are in a vivid and imaginary dream, intuition and information that is beyond our normal conscious awareness becomes accessible. It is also where we hold our emotional scars, our fears, all of our troubled history, and nightmares. Equally, it is where we also store all of our positive beliefs and habits. Theta brain waves are associated with increased learning memory, creativity and being in a deep state of meditation, and is the seat to the subconscious mind. If ever you've experienced an intuitive flash then that typically would happen when you're in a *Theta* frequency.

Children between the ages of 2 and 7 years of age operate in theta and usually live in their abstract world of imagination and at times will exhibit some nuances of critical and rational thinking. But more importantly during these years what we hear and experience affects our future self and our belief systems as we unconsciously absorb all that's around us and develop our subconscious behaviours. For example, 'money is the root of all evil', or 'boys don't cry'. These statements go straight to your subconscious mind seeing us have this love hate relationship with money when we get older, seeing us suppress emotions and act as though expressing the emotions to what affects us is a sign of weakness.

Aristotle said, *'Give me a boy until he is 7 and I will show you the man.'*

3. Alpha brain waves are dominant during the times when we have quietly flowing thoughts, and in some meditative states, it is the resting state for the brain. Alpha waves support our overall mental coordination, calmness, alertness, our mind-body integration and our learning. Alpha waves are associated with relaxation, wellbeing and have a tendency to be linked with increased levels of serotonin. We get into a brainwave activity state of *Alpha* when less stimulation is needed to be processed by our brains; as a result our brain relaxes and is when our brainwaves will begin to slow down. *Alpha* is when our inner world is more real than our outer world and is why it's referred to as our imaginary world and is the place of creativity. It's where we get our best ideas from.

In *Alpha* waves the brain will start to consolidate all of the sensory information you've just taken in and that's how you learn. Between the ages of 5 to 8 the analytical mind of a child starts to form and so the child starts to develop their own understanding of the life they've been exposed to. You will tend to find that children at this age believe their imaginary world is as real as the real world, for instance if you asked the child to pretend he or she was a cat, they would embrace that challenge and even hours later still assume that character. Comparatively an adult would laugh at you and think you were out of your mind for even asking.

4. Beta brain wave patterns are associated with alertness, concentration and learning, and that's because when you're thinking, your analytical brain, the 'neocortex', has to integrate all of the information that the senses are picking up and is constantly trying to create meaning of your environment and what you're focussing on. Beta brain waves are further divided into three bands; *'Low level Beta'*, which can be thought of as a 'fast idle', for example you're reading a book and taking in all the information. The second is *'Mid Level Beta'*, which is associated with a higher level of engagement. Or when you're actively figuring something out. For example, if I randomly told you that you were going to be tested on what you have just read. And lastly, *'High Level Beta'*, is when you've engaged in highly complex thought, integrating new experiences, high levels of anxiety and excitement. Being in a continual high frequency processing state is not a very efficient way to run the brain as it becomes incoherent and disorganised and is that's not the time for you to accept any new information. It is the main reason why we simply can't rationalise when we're heated.

When we're in high beta, we are usually living in an emergency mode.

Between the ages 8 to 12 we begin to develop our analytical mind and this is where we start to question whether things like Santa Claus are real. The brain will create a filter between the conscious and the unconscious mind. Remember, your conscious mind is only 5% of your total mind and is made up of logic and reasoning, your creative ability, your will and your faith. Your subconscious mind is made up of all the positive and negative identifications you've experienced throughout the first 12 years and the rest of your life. The subconscious mind is effectively 95% of who you are and is the gatekeeper of all your current habits and behaviours. But most importantly it is the same gatekeeper to your future self. The point is that if you're constantly living in high beta, then the information you desire to reprogram into your nervous system can't be processed, because you're on standby for any potential emergencies or environmental threats. It's the reason why it's been almost impossible to change some of the events you continue to find yourself manifesting and experiencing in life.

So the purpose of understanding your brain wave activity was to empower you with a level understanding of what state you're in, how you're responding and experiencing all the stimuli from your environment so that you can recognise what level of brain wave activity is needed in order to create the changes you desire in life. This whole journey isn't just about you learning about yourself but to also appreciate all the complex systems that have been put in place throughout our evolution, and how to use them all to your advantage to create what you do want rather than the same of what you don't want.

how the brain learns

'Implicit' vs. 'Explicit' Memories

In a podcast interview on brain performance Jay Shetty asked Dr Daniel Amen, 'what is the difference between the brain and the mind and what are the mistakes we make when talking about the mind versus understanding the brain?' Dr Daniel Amen's response was that the mind comes from the brain. It was a 90-minute podcast about *brain performance* and that's all he had on the mind. Those types of answers seem to be the same across all medical and science practices as there is no real definition for the mind. However, it's a concept we all use with phrases like, *'are you out of your mind?'* Or *'what's on your mind?'* We all seek *'peace of mind'* and we all use the term *'great minds think alike'*. I just find it funny that the mind is so profound yet no one really understands what it is.

Dr Joe Dispenza quotes that the mind is the brain in action and that if you change the way your brain works you're effectively changing your mind. I totally have to agree, the mind is the driving force behind the brain's intended action. The mind is associated with emotion, imagination, intelligence and most importantly our free will. There are two vital components that allow us to make the brain work in new ways and they are 'implicit memories' and 'explicit memories'. As we've now established, every time you learn something new there is a physical change in your brain. That's because the network of neurons that form your past habits or programs begin to untangle and the new program you're installing begins to take shape as the new networks of neurons begin to connect. Your brain cells genuinely want to develop long term relationships with each other all in the name of conserving energy and maintaining a high level of efficiency in the way you are able to process any type of stimuli. Before your brain feels the need to make any type of changes and create new synaptic connections, the brain must begin to trust that you are genuinely back in charge again, and so you will need to prove that this is your new preferred habit through consistency and repetition.

The fundamental difference between your learning and memory, is that learning is the acquisition of new knowledge or skills and your memory is *retention* of the learned information. The two ways the brain learns are through what is referred to as our explicit and implicit memories.

1. **'The Explicit Memory'** system begins to develop when we are around 18 months old. Our explicit memory system allows us to recreate the history of ourselves, it is verbal and conscious as we're able to think of the past experience and recall the details and the sequence of the events. Explicit memories are made up of facts and events which are split into two subgroups or categories, the first is *episodic memories* which are memories made up of our life's experiences. For example, we remember the first time our parents let us drive the car. Another example is that we remember our first kiss. The second is *semantic memories* which are memories of facts or knowledge. For example, you remember your friend's phone number. So in short the two types of explicit memories are knowledge (semantic) and experiences (episodic).

2. **'Implicit Memories'** are made up of skill or things we've repeated so many times, they've become autonomous and something we no longer need to think about. They are automatic, unconscious behaviours, unconscious attitudes and our unconscious emotional reactions. It is a process that happens without the need for thought; they're referred to as 'procedural memories'. In short, it's when you're able to perform a task without thinking about

it and is in our unconscious recollection of an action, for example riding a bike. Our implicit memory system will continue to develop throughout our entire lives; however, it's said that the most impressionable years are from when we're born up until we're about 7 years of age. Which makes it essential for our children or any loved ones in their growing years that we create an environment where this implicit memory system can take on the information and experiences about how the world works so that their actions reflect the life they desire; because the implicit memory system is largely why we keep defaulting back to our past habits and behaviours.

Understanding the significance that your past perceptions and experiences have had and how they've shaped your thoughts and memories about who you are and what you experience, which then dictated a certain choice of action and ultimately become the catalyst to how you chose to experience your life will now help make it easier for you to change the lens of your past experiences so that they don't continue to paralyse your future ones.

Again if you can invest the time and effort into repeating the things you do want over and over again, there will come a time where your brain cells will set together and develop stronger connections to all the new programs that you wish to reflect in your new life and welcomed experiences.

author's message

Remember that the conscious mind is the cornerstone of our personality and when it is balanced it allows us to live out our lives in control of our environment, and more importantly, the subconscious mind. Without balance the conscious mind will be filled with doubt and negativity and that's when the subconscious mind will immediately take over and control how your conscious mind behaves. When the subconscious mind takes control of the reins you will tend to become irrational and at times feel like you're going insane. That is because the subconscious and conscious minds are not in sync and completely out of coherence.

For the best parts of our day we spend most of our time focussing on the stimulus from our external environment and we predominantly operate in any of the three levels of beta. The intention of this chapter was to help you facilitate moving out of the higher frequency beta brain waves and into a more coherent state, like alpha. And the ultimate goal is for you to bring yourself into a state of theta brainwaves so that you can finally become the creator of your environment.

If you continue to live in emergency mode the rest of your life how will you ever be able to create the changes you desire? It'd be impossible and that's because you'd be living in a continued 'fight or flight state' and experiencing all the normal associated behaviours of being in that state. This impacts your physiological state and negatively influences your perceptions, behaviours, attitudes and emotions in a way that reflects a mindset state where you allow your external environment to dictate how you think, act and feel. That's when the reactive, unstable and volatile patterns of the brain begin to head down the road to a dead end of chronic fatigue, anxiety and depression. The idea is you now want to create an environment that allows you to add the programs that will help you live out the rest of your life on your terms, that's when you can genuinely go from being the victim to being the victor.

III

Your new understanding of
how it is we learn and what brain
wave patterns that will allow you
to speak directly to the subconscious
mind has just become a game
changer and given you the power
to take back what's yours.
~ Your Life!

IIIIIIIIIIIIIIIIIIIIIIIIIIIIIIIIIIIIIIIIIIIIIIIIIIIII

chapter 6:
stress

Everybody worries, some worry all the time whilst others worry only sometimes. Worrying and stress get such a bad rap and that's simply because we don't understand them well enough, nor do we use them to our advantage.

Aristotle wrote in his book, *On Rhetoric* that life is about being and becoming; and by that he meant that who we are today is not necessarily who we become tomorrow. I pray that after you've completely read this chapter you too realise that without confusion, tension and frustration there is no growth. It's through confusion, it's through our challenges that we find the inspiration to search deeper. Obstacles we encounter end up being the catalyst to a deeper and meaningful life, because when we're overly content and satisfied we never look deep enough. So the frustrations we end up enduring serve as a reminder that there is something more profound in respects to our abilities, achievement and life purpose.

The best thing is that it doesn't matter how long you have suffered from any of the nervous illnesses like anxiety or depression, if you wish to recover, then you can. You no longer need to commit to the disturbing memories of your past experiences and those unrelenting triggers.

It's your perceptions about the experiences that have kept you anchored to the emotions of the past that can be changed; and so I **challenge you** to apply all the components and the newfound wisdom you're now learning about. That is when you will finally improve your mental, physical and emotional health. I **challenge you** to finally take control of how you perceive your environment and realise that you are in total control of the outcomes you desire to manifest. I **challenge you** to think outside the box of conventional wisdom and allow yourself to accept the fact that worry and stress can just as easily have profound and positive impacts on who you are and who you're destined to become.

When you try and change I assure you you'll be challenged by your subconscious programs and at times you may feel like this is too hard. Remind yourself that strength cannot be born from strength, that strength can only be born from weakness. So embrace your momentary weaknesses as an opportunity to create incredible strength. Under constant strain of being in a stressed, anxious and depressed state you usually find that your heart beats quicker and yet you'll interpret it as a missed beat and may even seek medical intervention. You may even feel suffocated as you lack the ability to take deep breaths, yet you'll mistake it for being unfit. You may even experience feelings of headaches, nausea, stomach cramps and even diarrhea. All of what you're experiencing are normal symptoms of over stressing, isn't it time you stopped these symptoms from forming into life restricting patterns. The most amazing thing is all it takes is one idea of how you see the situation that you're stressing about to change it, the shift in how you see that situation will have the most profound impact in what behaviour you choose to express and to handle it.

A little story to put things in perspective. I know of someone who has a fear of being around a lot of people. She was socially anxious and after a short while it was starting to become a little overwhelming for her, so I escorted her outside so that she could breathe and relax. Literally within minutes she did, I then asked her why she was now able to relax when literally moments ago she was starting to spiral out of control? Her reply was that she now felt different and was why she could relax. I said this may be true, but what might be truer is that you're actually thinking differently out here than in there.

how the brain performs under stress

Stress isn't always a bad thing, short term it can give you some incredible benefits. Like enhancing short term focus and giving you a boost of energy or even better it can improve your physical abilities, for example if you're an athlete and engage in competitive sports. The issue is that when your stress responses are continuous, and when these stress response patterns begin to repeat themselves day in and day out the impacts on your brain can become that significant that it actually starts to change your brain. Chronic stress is known to affect the size of your brain, it's also known to affect its structure and how the brain actually functions. When we ruminate and begin to allow negative emotions to control us there is an immediate increase of neural activity in the *amygdala*, which is known as the *'brain's fear centre'*; that's when a surge of the stress hormone *'cortisol'* is released into the body, which signals the body to perk up and be on standby to run from any potential environmental threats. As our cortisol levels continue to rise then the level of neural activity in the *hippocampus* region of the brain will begin to deteriorate, which is the part of the brain that is responsible for learning, memory and stress control.

Again the worst thing is that having continued elevated levels of cortisol will begin to shrink the size of your brain, and if you're shrinking your brain then you're also reducing the amount of synaptic connections that you have. When parts of the brain like the 'prefrontal cortex' shrink, the consequence is it starts to affect how well we concentrate, it affects our decision-making abilities, it also affects our judgement and how well we interact socially. This process of chronic stress and its impacts on the brain has also been linked with being a potential precursor to things like depression and Alzheimer's disease. In short, being in a constant stressful state will modulate your adrenalin, increase your heart rate, reduce your IQ by up to 50 percent and worse can reduce the size of your brain, and is why we say and do all the dumbest things when we're stressed.

good stress vs. bad stress

If you think of the worst and get the worst then you suffer twice, if you think of the best and get the worst then you only suffer once. The issue is that most of us unconsciously love to suffer.

Stress is a natural occurrence that the human body needs to live and that's simply because we are a stimulus response organism, we are designed to respond to the stimulus that comes at us. That's basically what stress is. Everybody can handle pressure; most people decide not to. The issue is that we often think of stress as a bad thing, however, the truth is if you try and live a stress-free life then it won't take long before you realise that you're actually not living, you would be too complacent to go out and do anything. As a result there'd be no growth in your life, which makes *'stress'* a valuable commodity.

There are two main forms of stress: 'Activated stress' known as good stress and 'Inhibited stress' which is the bad stress. To put things into perspective, imagine a lion chasing a gazelle, the lion is experiencing all the symptoms of good 'activated' stress, which is usually short term and it drives you to go after whatever it is you desire. The gazelle on the other hand is experiencing the bad 'inhibited' stress and does whatever it can to survive, much like how the world and the human race has evolved; since the day of our creation we have only grown and will only continue to grow because of stress, even that gazelle. Our problem is we believe our lives are so stressful, meaning, that we believe we cannot deal with our reality of life. So the first thing we usually do without realising is hold our breath, as it's a fear response, which in return accelerates our fight or flight response. If you think about it logically, stress is pressure you won't deal with, or that you don't have the tools to deal with yet; and if your way of dealing with it is to avoid the pressure situation, what you will find is that another one will come along, and then another one comes along until you're dealing with stress. Remember the problem is only a problem when you decide not to deal with it, you'll soon see that it's usually your philosophy that's the issue and not the problem itself.

A little story to put the significance and importance of stress and being uncomfortable for growth to happen in perspective. Lobsters are a soft creature and live inside a shell, this shell is crucial for the lobsters' survival, yet it does not expand. As the lobster grows, the shell now becomes quite uncomfortable and restrictive. That is when the lobster will cast off that shell and produce another one so that it can continue to grow, until that shell also becomes uncomfortable and restrictive. Again that is when the lobster will seek protection from its predators and will cast off that shell and produce another one.

Throughout the lobster's life it repeats this process about 25 times. The point of this short story is that the stimulus for the lobster to continue to grow is that it must be uncomfortable first. When you can teach yourself to look at a stressful situation as an opportunity to grow and transform your stress into this positive energy that inspires your personal fulfillment, that is when you can truly be the creator of your environment. The intended message here is that the same stressful situations that have caused you fear and kept you anchored in a constant anxious state have the potential to improve your quality of life mentally, physically and emotionally; and that even the precious diamond originates as coal, but with the aid of the immense pressure that it is placed under in nature is eventually transformed it into the queen of all gems.

anxiety

Anxiety is associated with one of our most primal instincts to avoid threats, only the difference now is that we've now given a title to what was once known as a rush or a feeling. Every time anxiety comes up in a conversation, there is always a negative association with it; the truth is that anxiety is a surge of energy caused by an emotion or feeling. As outlined in previous chapters, thoughts create their relevant emotion and those emotions create feelings, which are then associated with its particular biochemical reaction. In no way am I dismissing any of your traumatic events nor would I ever ask you to dismiss them yourself; the intent is to empower you with a new perspective, with new choices, a brand-new way of applying that excess energy. By applying the wisdom of your newfound knowledge, you will no doubt develop the tools and the understanding to better deal with whatever traumatic experiences that have kept you anchored in the past.

We humans tend to focus on negativity, simply because our biology and evolution have hard wired us that way. This is sometimes called Negative Bias. This was very necessary during our evolution. The constant anxiety that cave men lived with helped them to stay alert and more importantly, alive. This type of belief system has become so hardwired into our DNA that we've lost the ability to focus on growth and have instead been scared into a constant survival mode. One of many examples would be when you turn the television on in the morning and watch the news, you're now primed for a day of negativity with the media's mantra being, *'if it bleeds it leads'*. All this is doing is reinforcing this negative loop known as the Negative Bias.

Do you remember when you would come home from school with your report card and say, 'mum, dad, I got three 'A's!' Your mother would take the report card and highlight how you also got a 'C'. Or if you're walking with two friends and one pays you a compliment, for example, 'I love your shoes.' But the other somehow feels the need to highlight something negative and says 'yeah, but why do you walk like that?' You would spend the rest of the day replaying that negative remark instead of the compliment. That's simply because *negative* is stronger than the *positive*. A negative thing may happen and we immediately react and begin to stress. We continue to think about that experience then stress even more. The brain eventually recognises this pattern and begins to set itself in place to seek out another negative event. And so it begins to scan your day looking for moments or events to reinforce your current belief and emotion. Even though throughout the day there were positive situations that happened, your reticular activating system (RAS) thought all the positive events were not important enough to focus on because they didn't resonate with your current belief. It chose to highlight anything that would keep you in your current state of mind. This is the kind of toxic negative cycle that not only affects you and your health; it also affects your children, your spouse, loved ones and family.

Your perspective on anxiety has the power to shape how it impacts you. A recent study in the *Journal of Individual Differences* found that participants who viewed stressful events as challenges, rather than threats, gained a boost in energy from their anxiety. As a result their performance improved dramatically, as the science of anxiety continues to evolve, a lot more is being understood about anxiety's role in how it helps protect a person as well as motivate optimal behaviour, despite its common reputation for being a problematic symptom.

I guess what I am saying is if you can use it to your advantage then there stands to be so much to gain from how you deal with your anxious state of mind. Equally, if you allow it to escalate quickly and control you, then you will continue to suffer for the rest of your life. A way to change problematic feelings that lead to paralysing and debilitating anxiety is to change the associated thoughts, which inevitably leads to changing your actions because thoughts create feelings that dictate an action. The fear and perceived possibility of a bad thing happening is usually twice as bad as if the real fear actually happened and that's because whenever we anticipate anything, the thoughts we project and create will always be an extreme version, especially as your rational and thinking brain is the first to go offline when you enter a heightened state of being.

Anxiety is usually triggered by some sort of undigested trauma, that seems to be at the forefront of every moment. You meet it with an expectation, a fear and at times some sort of resignation. What that means is that your past experience makes you over determine the present moment and so you begin to create in your mind a future experience that you can identify with; a process referred to by psychologists as 'cognitive distortion', a negative exaggeration that has become a habitual and an unconscious way of thinking that is not realistic. If you grew up with a parent who constantly expected the worse from every situation, then you might have just assumed this was the way to see the world. Or if you had a difficult period of your life that left you feeling helpless, that these past traumatic experiences and anxieties now becomes something you unconsciously use to try and make yourself feel less disappointed when something doesn't go right. We adopt this type of mindset as a protective mechanism in order to better deal with disappointments or expected trauma because we've been overwhelmed by those experiences in the past. Who wants to be disappointed again? It's easier to assume the worst and sabotage than it is to potentially be hurt and let down again. All this does is allow you to live a life that is unlived and keep you anchored in a state that is familiar with those traumas.

When you're able to finally make sense of all this, you'll find it much easier to change the outcomes of any situation. And the reason for that is that when you learn anything new that can change your perception. What is really happening is that your *subjective mind* now meets the *objective truth*, and in that moment there will be a revelation that highlights a brand-new ecstatic type of experience that you'll translate into some sort of a victory. You've just conquered or faced and overcome something that would usually make you run in fear. As soon as you adopt this brand new and empowered growth mindset, then the sooner it will result in you looking for the next opportunity where you can apply this newfound knowledge and so you make the most out of every moment to learn and grow.

The final message here is that the next time you experience the anxious rush of a perceived danger, remember that by dealing with the variable in the present moment without the rumination and paralysing thoughts that the conscious mind is able to conjure up, that you will no doubt develop the resilience to better deal with any stressful situation. The idea is to be in the moment, to be present and deal with it the best way you can, and that even though you didn't succeed in overcoming the circumstance be proud that you faced it and didn't run and if you continue to do that then I promise that there will come a time where you develop a resilience and strength that can't be taught in any textbooks.

So if you can make an active choice to use your agitation or the energy that anxiety creates towards your desired and creative purpose and repeat that process again, and then again, there will come a time when your body begins to understand that this energy is leverage in being able to get things done. And so this energy no longer brings with it a series of negative imprints but rather a new outlook that is associated with being proactive and productive.

Successful people today use that same survival tool and channel that energy towards creating their desired outcome and when you're able to shift your perception and apply intent then stress and anxiety becomes a very powerful commodity.

depression

Depression is a mental health disorder characterised by a persistently depressed mood or loss of interest in activities, causing significant impairment in daily life, according to the description.

Of all the species of mammals we're born the most vulnerable. Other mammals are born and within minutes are adapting to their environment and walking; yet here we are capable of building rocket ships but when we're born we basically just lay there helpless and cry, dependant on our parents for love and protection. Just as importantly, we also need to feel psychologically safe. Our psychological needs are that we must feel as though we belong, that our lives have a purpose and that we are valued; most importantly we need to feel like we have a future that makes sense. We now live in an era that has become fixated on creating technological breakthrough after breakthrough and we've forgotten to meet our deep and underlying psychological needs. I believe that this is a *key player* in the rise of the depression epidemic. Granted, that's not the only cause, however, there are a plethora of studies in medical journals that back this claim up highlighting the fact that having a lower sense of belonging was significantly associated with a greater severity of depression, hopelessness, and suicidal ideation; and that a *'Sense'* of belonging displayed a significant and critical role in the recovery from depression and hopelessness. I believe that for any medical practitioner to say that all depression is only caused by having low levels of serotonin can be misleading.

Here is something you may not have considered. Can you be depressed and not have depression? The point is that at times you may think you have depression, but what you have is a *feeling* of being depressed. This is quite normal if the circumstance requires some form of grieving in order to best process whatever situation you are experiencing. But you insist on visiting the doctor and disclose your symptoms and what you're feeling, the doctor punches in those symptoms into the computer and the ultimate diagnosis is that you have depression. With so many patients in a typically overloaded healthcare system, it's no wonder that sometimes it's easier to give someone a pill rather than invest the time to educate them and give them tools to manage how they process their state of being. There is a genuine difference between being in a 'depressed state' or 'suffering from depression' and that is that there can be a feeling of depression. For example, if you have suffered the loss of a loved one, which brings with it realistic feelings of grief. In that instance being in a depressed state isn't an illness and is considered by psychiatrists a normal part of the grieving process. It's actually quite healthy to process your emotions and grieve. Unfortunately, most people will suppress that grief because it's too painful to process and discuss. Which then turns into a depressive state of being and in this instance an *antidepressant* more than likely won't change that until you're ready to process the emotions that have been contributing to your state of depression and deal with them properly.

The second part to this nuance is that there could be a problem that lies within your biochemical systems, and that is when it isn't producing enough serotonin which is a neurotransmitter that helps regulate mood, happiness and affects the way we feel. This is when medical intervention may be what is best prescribed until you are able to improve your overall health and wellbeing. The point here is that if you have neurohormone imbalances they will trigger feelings of severe depression and despair; these imbalances can be either hereditary or can be triggered by poor health and lifestyle. Or they can be generated by your subjective perceptions that have now become your default thinking and what you are inevitably focussing on and manifesting.

My suggestion is to see a specialist if at any time you feel like you're severely depressed, out of control, or suicidal, until you're able to better manage your state of depression. However having any sort of depression could be triggered by an imbalance in any one of the Six Pillars outlined in coming chapters and by being able to identify them and utilise the tools that you will acquire, then this will allow you to easily implement a management plan that will improve your overall health and wellbeing including your state of depression. The message here is that not everyone needs the same treatment and medical intervention isn't the only solution, and that one should really try and understand what the nature of their depression is so that they are able to approach it in the most appropriate manner instead of relying on antidepressants, because they are insidious and will alter the way your brain works to now rely on the medication.

In the upcoming chapters I will be going into much greater detail about the Six Pillars that you can use in your daily life. When you use these balanced strategies you will be able to improve your overall health, wellbeing and your mental state.

According to the World Health Organization, depression is now the most common worldwide illness with one out of every four people suffering from any one of the symptoms of depression, and an astounding 1 person every 40 seconds commits suicide globally.

So why are we so sad? Statistics isn't something I really wanted to focus on but this is such a significant number and the fact that a staggering amount of *Human Beings* feel the need to take their lives when all they may have needed was someone to turn the light on in their dark room and show them that they have every opportunity to change, is heartbreaking. This is why I have obsessed about figuring out a way to shed some light on how best to transform your depression into exhilaration.

I believe it's because the story we tell ourselves about ourselves is no longer convincing or serving us our purpose. So what does it really mean to be depressed? Psychiatrists describe depression as a set of stories with excessive rumination of the autobiographical mind, which is a memory system consisting of episodes recollected from an individual's life, based on a combination of episodic memories (personal experiences and specific objects, people and events experienced at a particular time and place), and semantic memories (general knowledge and facts about the world). As has been outlined, what we choose to remember isn't what we always think actually happened. This excessive rumination is influenced by our ego, which is designed to get us to act with intent and agency in order for us to keep evolving, creating, and so that we get things done. In short, we've lost our way and we're now longing for something to remind us of who we are and what it is we're meant to do.

I believe to some degree that our misinterpretation of what anxiety is and how it can be best utilised has contributed to the development of the depression epidemic. Anxiety and emotions helped us stay alive and without them both we may not have survived. Humans will always crave a sense of belonging, as it is hardwired into our DNA. Although technology has become exceptionally advanced in this field, this *innate evolutionary primitive program* has become neglected. It's almost as though we have been seduced into this distant and anti-social type of reality. Do you remember when we were children we were never afraid to be ourselves? We were passionate, creative and inquisitive. We wanted to be rock stars or even astronauts. We dared to dream as the fulfilment of our aspirations gave our lives meaning. As we transitioned from the perfection of childhood along the way we hear *'No!'*, *'that's not a practical dream'*, *'go to school to study and then work hard and pay off your house'*. It has been drilled into our subconscious mind, to create a life that lacks any type of personal meaning and that we must do what is expected and not what we love. The inevitable is a certain level of conformity that begins to control our every decision for the rest of our lives.

I can honestly empathise as I too have had my crisis of meaning in life and experienced my fair share of anxiousness, and at times suffocated in my own distress. So I make no judgements, all I wish to do is shed some light on why it is, that we as a race, are becoming so sad so that we learn how to move away from these triggers and transform them into a state of empowerment no longer allowing them to control us. This untold power in knowing then doing will soon liberate you and no longer allow you to be controlled by these triggers and spiral out of control ever again. I guess what I am saying is that we will never eradicate anxiety or feelings of being depressed because they are very relevant to the cycle of who we are and what we become, and so I cannot guarantee that you will never be hurt or upset again, but I can guarantee that you never allow it to control you and suck the life right out of you.

A little story to help you see that most times all that is needed is for you to change your perspective about yourself and that if you look hard enough you'll see that you actually have a purpose and maybe more. There was this villager who would place a pole across his shoulders that had a massive clay pot on either end. This villager used this to carry water back home from the well, one of the clay pots had cracks in it and the other didn't. Every time the villager would get home, the clay pot with the cracks in it would feel like a liability and worthless because the clay pot would only return half full, yet the other one was completely full.

This process repeated itself for years and had the cracked clay pot confused. So one day he summoned the courage to confront the villager and asked him, 'Master! Why is it you continue to carry me, I am a liability to you, why haven't you replaced me?' The villager looked at the pot and paused for a moment before replying, 'I always knew you had these cracks, yet what you saw as a liability I saw as an opportunity. Tomorrow on our journey back home from the well, please observe the impact your cracks have had on your side of the trail.'

So as his master wished, the cracked pot observed the path on the way home from the well. To his surprise his side of the path was filled with the most amazing and vibrant flowers. The master then turned to the cracked pot and said, 'You see. I knew you had cracks and so I planted seeds on your side to help make the journey home a delight.' A lesson here is that we all have something that at times may appear as a setback, or something we must face that may appear too daunting or impossible. And with the right mindset and a clearer outlook and changed perception, those setbacks or circumstances in life can turn out to have the most powerful purpose.

If you change your focus and psychology then there is a strong chance you can change your state of being, in other words if you change the meaning then you can change the thoughts, feelings and emotions.

order and chaos

||||||||||||||||||||||||||||||||||||||||||||||||||||||||||

You need Chaos in your soul,
to give birth to a dancing star.
~ Friedrich Nietzsche

||||||||||||||||||||||||||||||||||||||||||||||||||||||||||

The meaning of *'Chaos'* that I am referring to is anything that is unknown or any unexplored territory. *Chaos* is when we don't know what we are doing or what is happening. Chaos is the catastrophe that will suddenly enter our life. *Chaos* is the potential for growth and is something we can call on when our perceptual order is doing us an injustice. The important point here is that chaos is a permanent element of our existence and why we can never avoid it.

On the other side of this spectrum is *Order*. When we are in order the behaviour of our environment matches our expectations. When we are certain of everything then we are in order. The issue is, how do we know that our perceptual order is the best kind of order for us? The truth is we don't. Because we don't know everything, and therefore everything we do or choose is bound to a certain level of bias or ignorance. That's why the presence of chaos is extremely important as it will challenge our perceptions. And every time we experience a certain level of turbulence and then deal with it then the end result will be some level of growth. As we continue to develop an understanding about our personal likes and dislikes then our personal order will also continue to progress and evolve. Throughout our lives we experience certain levels of catastrophe and that is because all things will continue to evolve and change, much as our environment and expectations has changed throughout the course of our lives. It's with the presence of chaos that we find ourselves developing a new level of perceptual order. For example, you graduate from school thinking that you wanted to be an accountant, you start working and realise that accounting is not what you like anymore and so now you are stuck looking for what you feel best resonates with you. If you think that where you are in life is the perfect order, then I dare you to try and remain there. What you will find is that sooner or later disorder will eventually enter your life all by itself and that's when your 'ideal static structure' is destined to fail and that's because the world is in constant motion and history has taught us that nothing remains the same.

Having only order in your life will quickly begin holding you back from new possibilities and opportunities. Equally, having too much chaos will become unbearable, overwhelming and create certain levels of fear, so the idea is that you want to live out your life with one foot on the things you have learnt and mastered and the other foot exploring and mastering new experiences. Dr Jordan Peterson highlights in his teachings that the best way of conceptualising meaningful reality is by intentionally living on the border of order and chaos. Could you imagine how boring your life would be if it is all in order and you could predict everything? Tell me that you wouldn't eventually become bored by that level of security? There would be no new information, no growth, it would be exactly the same as wearing the exact same outfit every day for the rest of your life.

The message here is that as you continue to learn and grow that you don't ever settle because you are capable of whatever you desire in life. If you wish to grow you must embrace life's challenges. Imagine the ubiquitous *Yin* and *Yang* symbol for a moment. It is a symbol of the totality of both duality and balance, which is exactly what we are talking about, it is a concept that will allow you to genuinely experience yourself and inevitably learn and grow as the two sides of the Yin and Yang symbol represents both order and chaos.

The idea is that there is this mutual coexistence that makes up our world, that comprises a side that has a feminine, black serpent represented with a white dot. And on the other side is a white, masculine serpent with a black dot, the dots indicate the potential of transformation. They're connected head to tail which is a representation that there can be neither without each other. Each environment that you're in will always be composed of things you understand and things that you don't understand, which basically sums up the existential process of human beings and life. So by placing yourself right on the border between order and chaos you only stand to get the best of both worlds as they genuinely are the fundamental elements to every living thing in our existence.

'In the midst of chaos, there is also opportunity.'
~ Sun Tzu

chapter 7:
the first pillar – movement

In modern life we are now predisposed to a sedentary lifestyle which deems our society one that is physically inactive and one that spends a large amount of time in a sitting position. According to the World Health Organization, the sedentary lifestyle and physical inactivity have become an epidemic.

We all need to remember that we are living in our bodies and we were designed to move and adapt. The body is this amazing intelligence that is constantly adapting to what we do and don't do, always scanning itself, figuring out what is not working properly, then finds reinforcement from other muscles and joints all in the name of keeping you alive. The intention of this chapter is to remind you of the myriad of your functionality and to help you redefine your physicality and how you look at movement. I'm sure we've all heard the saying that 'our bodies are our temples'. What that really means is that we have a physical existence, and so my question to you is how can you ignore it and not have the urge to explore your true physical potential and all the benefits associated with movement itself? Science is only starting to discover the importance of movement and how it is the precursor to improving brain function, learning and overall health.

You see we were created and designed to move, we are opportunistic movers and streamlined and designed for multi-joint, multi-plane, dynamic movement against the force of gravity over distance.

How does it feel to know that you are a system of integrated systems that only operate best in the presence of movement? The sad thing is that we as a race have become the weakened warriors; the body and mind are one big kinetic chain and there's no real isolated existence of one without the other. Throughout this chapter, you'll soon see that movement is an integral part of genuinely improving your mental, physical and emotional health. Up until this day and age most people would associate exercise and movement as beneficial for only improving your cardiovascular health and for losing weight. If that has been your belief then it may just be time to learn the truth.

There was an article in *Time* magazine where a doctor stated that if there were a drug that could do for human health what movement can, then it would be the most valuable pharmaceutical developed. Having said that, it's obvious we need to start understanding how movement affects the brain. Neuroscientist Dr Daniel Wolpert suggested that,

'We have a brain for one reason only and that's to use adaptable and complex movements'. Process that for a moment, everything that the brain facilitates other than thinking is a form of movement, communicating, emotional expression, language and the list goes on. The new research on exercise and movement allows us to gain a better understanding of neurochemical mechanisms and their strong connection between the brain and movement, to where a bigger brain is needed to facilitate complex movements. If you combine the complex movements with increasing your heart rate then that will amplify your brain power tenfold, so that we start to learn more efficiently, better deal with stress whilst improving and managing anxiety.

Up until three decades ago it was thought or assumed that whatever brain cells that you were born with was all that you had and now neuroscientists have worked out that's not the case. In the hippocampus region of the brain we can now stimulate the growth of regeneration of nerve cells through a process called neurogenesis. Neurogenesis broken down means nerve cells or brain cells plus conversion or formation. Regular workouts or committing to being active can be applied to everything in life and it creates discipline.

Nothing comes without training, not even a great relationship. For example, by consistently completing and marking off a workout on the *Body By Michael* App (see the projectyou.tv website for details). or anyone of your preferred apps, this will develop better discipline. Especially when you start the day by having one of those empowering wins by overcoming any subconscious sabotage. This win will put you in control of yourself and in control of your day. There is nothing more rewarding than starting your day off being bigger than your own excuses.

neurogenesis and movement

IIIIIIIIIIIIIIIIIIIIIIIIIIIIIIIIIIIIIIIIIIIIIIIIIIIIII

'When your Body moves
your Brain grooves'

IIIIIIIIIIIIIIIIIIIIIIIIIIIIIIIIIIIIIIIIIIIIIIIIIIIIII

Up until three decades ago it was thought that most of the development of the brain happened up until the early 20s, when our brains stopped growing and we stopped producing new brain cells.

In the late 1990s scientists realised that the brain makes new brain cells throughout our entire lives. This new phenomena is called neurogenesis, **Neuro** meaning nerve cells or brain cells and **Genesis** meaning conversion or formation.

Science refers to a process known as brain plasticity whereby every time we change the way we think and feel we actually change the shape of the brain. The hippocampus region of the brain is responsible for learning and retaining new knowledge and the size of it is directly related to the amount of neurogenesis, more importantly the rate of neurogenesis has been found to have a huge impact on our lives. For example, a lower rate of neurogenesis is associated with cognitive decline, memory problems, anxiety and depression. By contrast a higher rate of neurogenesis is associated with rapid learning, cognitive enhancement, and best of all, an emotional resilience.

Neurogenesis has many facets to it and if you can approach it using all the levels, then the impact is so much more profound. Each of the core Six Pillars that you're about to learn about impacts the production of neurogenesis positively. The reason is that every level of consciousness comes to us via the brain, so the quality of our brain is really determined by the quality of our lives. Implementing them in a structured program will create subtle yet the most profound shifts you could ever imagine.

Being that socially we have become prone to a neurotoxic lifestyle, we really want to stop repeating the things that slow down the production of new brain cells and focus on what will enhance it. All forms of physical activity have profound impacts and benefits for the body and the mind. However, for you to maximise the proliferation of new brain cells you must increase your heart rate whilst being active. For example, explosive type functional movements are amazing for increasing the rate of neurogenesis. Every time we learn something new there is a physical change that goes on in our brains, learning a new movement pattern stimulates so much activity in the brain as well as enhancing the process of neurogenesis. There are three phases to learning a new movement pattern.

Phase one is learning something completely new where you feel uncoordinated, become frustrated and have a tendency to want to give up. *Phase two* is improving on the movement pattern that you have just learnt. *Phase three* is perfecting the movement pattern you've just learnt. The idea is that we need to be in all three phases every day, perfecting something that we learnt a while ago, improving something that we recently learnt and learning something new every day. Can you imagine how much neurological stimulation one would get by having to recruit these new motor patterns on a daily basis? That's why one of the reasons dancers can be so eccentric and creative, is that they could learn hundreds of new movement patterns every time they learn a new routine.

There's one other important fact to consider when you commit to being active with regular workouts. It creates discipline. It's those empowering wins, that moment of wow! *I can't believe I just completed this workout.* And then marking it off as complete that gives you that sense of you conquering something before the day starts, that can only translate into you looking for more things to conquer. You now start the day with confidence. That new self-confidence will now be translated into you thinking and feeling differently about yourself. The best part of it is that your physiology will also change with a more commanding energy as you stand nice and tall and proud.

By committing to being more active can you see the ripple effect that stems deeper than just working out to lose weight. By having small victories throughout the day, it'll prime your mind for success. Look at it as an opportunity rather than an issue or a problem. All of these victories will now re-conceptualise your internal narrative.

movement and mood

The fundamentals of this pillar isn't about how fit you are or how big your muscles are. Sure they're both things to aspire towards improving every time you work out or by intentionally living out an active lifestyle. Generally people who exercise and have an active lifestyle find that they have an improved sense of well-being, they feel more energetic throughout the day, sleep better at night, have sharper memories, and most importantly feel positive about themselves and their lives. In the Journal of Clinical Psychiatry there was an article about exercise for mental health that focussed on the exponential growth of the 'metabolic syndrome' and obesity and found that the most cost-effective way to improve mental, physical and psychological health was a lifestyle modification that incorporates physical activity. The study was focussed on individuals that are at a high risk of chronic diseases associated with sedentary behaviour and medication side effects, for example, diabetes, hyperlipidaemia, and cardiovascular diseases.

The ultimate finding was that movement and exercise were the essential components and the most practical and suitable lifestyle modification. The importance of exercise is not adequately understood or appreciated by patients and mental health professionals alike. Evidence has suggested that exercise may be an often-neglected intervention in mental health care. It's funny that it's overlooked when the scientific evidence shows that things like aerobic exercises, jogging, swimming, cycling, walking, gardening, and dancing, have all been shown to reduce anxiety and depression. The improvements in mood are induced because of the increase in blood circulation to the brain, which ultimately leaves a positive influence on the physiologic reactivity to stress and stresses in general.

Most of us are aware of what happens to the body when we exercise. We build more muscle and increase our stamina. Unfortunately, it's usually the last reason we choose to be active and exercise when it comes to our brain, yet the benefits are profound on our cognitive function, our mental state and mood.

Since I could remember every time I would ask random people that approach me at gyms why they work out, the immediate response would be, ' they love the endorphins rush they get as it makes them feel amazing' without knowing it they were onto something. Endorphins are hormones that are produced by your central nervous system and a part of the brain known as the pituitary gland, that work together with the intent to inhibit the transmission of any pain signals. The by-product of this just so happens to be a feeling of euphoria, this is what makes you feel happier instantly with the effects lasting a good amount of time.

During specific moments of exercising and being active your body will also secrete other hormones like serotonin, norepinephrine, BDNF (Brain-Derived Neurotrophic Factor) and dopamine. The combination of these five neurotransmitters can boost your mood, and more importantly have been proven to help manage and relieve both anxiety and depression. The BDNF has a protective and also reparative element to your memory neurons and acts as a reset switch and is why we can often feel so at ease, that things are clear after exercising and that we are eventually happy.

Lastly, movement and exercise not only improve your mood but they have now scientifically been proven to help to preserve brain function and prevent cognitive decline.

flexibility, mobility and pliability

We live in an era where information is easily accessible and buzzwords are constantly thrown around creating confusion all in an attempt to get fancy. What you'll learn is that in no way do we need to get fancy but rather get effective. By becoming effective you'll be able to address so much more in the same amount of time. A huge misconception is that most people assume that the terms flexibility and mobility are interchangeable and that if you are flexible you are automatically mobile. Although flexibility is a component of mobility, mobility and flexibility are different.

Here's a thought, what's the use of being flexible and mobile if you're not functional? Our primal patterns include, pushing, pulling, squatting, lunging, bending, extending and gait (walking). How are you ever going to work out effectively if you can't function efficiently? So the intended focus will be on functionality, but first, take a look at the differences between flexibility and mobility.

Flexibility is the ability of a muscle to lengthen passively, which means without resistance. Mobility on the other hand is the ability of a joint to move actively through a pain free full range of motion. To put things in perspective, let's say a person attempts to touch their toes and is unable to do so. They'd usually blame the lack of range of motion on tightness and restriction in their hamstring, when in fact it could be a *mobility* issue that could stem from your hips or spine. I know this may sound a little confusing but bear with me it'll all make sense. Ultimately, the point I make here is that it's not only stretching our muscles that helps with and improves how we function.

We move in three planes of motion sagittal: (front to back), frontal (side to side) and transverse (rotational). Therefore, we need to consider thinking outside the box of conventional wisdom in order to function optimally.

The body is one very comprehensive kinetic system where there are linkages or patterns that are from left to right, front to back and even diagonally. The reason is quite simply that movement is in 'everything' we do; it's universal. Although both flexibility and mobility are super important, what's even more important and practical than both of those is the *'effectiveness and the speed or quickness'* in which your muscles respond and effectively increase both the flexibility and the range of motion, a term referred to as **'pliability'**. So instead of focussing on stretching muscles and at times over mobilising a joint by lengthening the muscle too much and creating imbalances, let's start focussing on the common goal between them all, which is 'functional movement'.

The body comprises four load points, which are the ankles, the knees, the hips and the shoulders. These joints line up. When they are balanced, your shoulders sit over the hips, the hips over the knees and your knees over your ankles. Once the integrity of these joints is restored it'll improve your functionality and there'll be no more need for a compensated movement.

Our sedentary lifestyle has robbed us of the load bearing alignment and no matter how much we stretch and attempt to mobilise we'll never be able to move pain free unless we focus on them first. Think about how important these load joints are, sitting, standing, squatting, lunging, every single primal function and position relies on these load bearing joints in order to execute the movement effectively.

Pain Free, written by Peter Egoscue is definitely a book I would recommend you read. We will be focussing on seven static positions from his book that I feel is best suited for a general calibration process, these are simple and can be done right before bed or whilst you watch TV. If you can whilst you perform the sequence imagine your bones realigning themselves, breathe deep into the position, close your eyes and visualise your joints effortlessly falling back into place. Last point for you to take on board is that the most joint pain you will ever experience is because of the position of the joint capsule and not so much the condition of the joint capsule.

1. Gravity Drop
2. Static Back
3. Supine Groin Stretch
4. Cats & Dogs
5. Counter Stretch
6. Modified Floor Block

And if you can, then finish off with a 7th one:

7. An AirBench

I would ask that you read the rest of the book before engaging in these static exercises which are explained at the end of this chapter. The reason is quite simple and that is you won't just be going through the motions of just doing the suggested exercise, you will be applying 'intent' and all your newfound awareness from each of the Six Pillars into these exercises. That is when you will embrace the fact that this is an opportunity to have an internal dialogue with your bioenergetic cells and let them know you're back in control and that you won't let them down anymore. This will accelerate the success tenfold.

the wisdom of being active and not exercising

The holy grail of losing weight is diet and exercise; it's at the forefront of every program, marketing fads or what is prescribed to you by a personal trainer. The idea is to help you redefine and replace those words with ones that matter. If you think about it logically most that use those terms are usually only in it for the short term. A quick fix and in no way are they sustainable. If they were, why is it that we're currently facing the world's largest epidemic of obesity and other diseases that are associated with obesity and a sedentary lifestyle.

Instead of focussing on exercise, which is quite intimidating for most, why not focus on working out as in being active, I'm not in any way attempting to be trivial, but rather only concerned with helping you change the not so positive mindset of being active to a more profound and empowered way of looking at being active, rather than having to face the drudgery and intimidation associated with exercise. All it takes is one idea of how you see a circumstance to change that circumstance.

Instead of associating being active with the conventional 'training at a gym for hours at a time by jumping from one machine to another', we now can change any associations with working out to quite simply being active, whether it be going for a walk or playing a game of basketball at the park, or kicking the footy with the children, or even following a quick 10-minute structured outdoor bodyweight program. Being active is so important because the more active you become the better the chances of improving your mobility and functionality will be. More importantly, the end game of adopting this new mindset and lifestyle is inevitably improved muscle tone and a healthier body weight.

We're said to be creatures of habit. By getting into a consistent habit of either a workout or being active, there will eventually come a time when this becomes your new default setting in your subconscious mind. By adding some sort of reward, for example, I get a massage at the end of every week, it will help you stay on track and solidify this new synaptic program of habit.

However, if your intention is to burn fat by working out and being active, then a great way to maximise fat burning potential and improve your metabolic rate is to take advantage of something called 'the metabolic afterburn' which is induced by the intensity of a workout rather than the duration. I've always said you can train intensive or you can train extensive, but you can't do the two together. To put things in perspective let's imagine two different athletes, one is a marathon runner and the other is a 100m sprinter. Both are athletes in their own right, but with two very different body types. The 100m sprinter's body is ripped, chiselled, lean and has a lot of muscle tone and definition. Their workouts are explosive and dynamic and are usually shorter durations. The long-distance runner on the other hand is usually lanky and lean with very little to no muscle tone and that's purely because muscle needs energy and for a long-distance runner it becomes a liability. The point here is that if you're on the treadmill for hours at a time and continue to complain about the lack of progress and lack of tone, this could be one of the reasons why.

One other reason why treadmills are a bad idea and boring, is that the metabolic stimulus goes down as your body adapts. For example, if you've been using the treadmill every day for a month at say 6 km per hour, you will only get a fraction of the benefits that you did when you first started. That's because we are designed to adapt and that is part of the survival system of the body.

The science is very clear that interval training (which means any type of short burst training) is ideal for burning the most amount of fat and preserving muscle tone in the shortest amount of time. High Intensity Interval Training (HIIT) refers to alternating between very intense short explosive periods followed by a slow pace recovery period. Compared to 'steady state cardio,' which is a moderate continual pace for a given period of time. In a 12-week study done between HIIT workouts at 20-minutes, 3 times per week and Steady State Cardio at 30-minutes 3 times per week, it was found that both resulted in some form of weight loss. The most interesting fact is that the HIIT workouts were seven times more effective in fat loss to which the participants of HIIT also found an improvement of overall muscle tone compared to the steady state cardio.

HIIT workouts are a much more effective way of working out and burning fat as they create a metabolic afterburn for hours long after you've finished your workout. The workouts do this by elevating EPOC (excess post-exercise oxygen consumption), creating a metabolic afterburn for up to 72 hours.

If you would like to try a HIIT workout then simply download *The Project You App* (projectyou.tv) as it has unlimited daily HIIT routines for you.

There still are some benefits to also implementing steady state cardio that are functional as they do translate to helping your central nervous system to improve your recovery. They can also build up your aerobic fitness, as well as the evening walk has been linked to helping you reduce your *cortisol level*.

So if you're able to get fitter, the more fat you will burn, because the general rule of thumb is that the more aerobically fit you are, the more oxygen you can use. The point of bringing up both benefits is so that if HIIT workouts are something that you feel you're not ready for or sound intimidating, then it doesn't hurt to start with steady state cardio or walking out in the park until you build your aerobic fitness and are confident enough to attempt a HIIT workout. Initially, either one will be beneficial for you.

When you do feel like you're ready to take on interval type training then your main focus is to increase your VO2 Max, as it will result in improving your fat burning potential and get to your goal a lot quicker. By keeping your workouts intense and the heart pumping as hard as is physically possible and practical for you, you will burn calories. The reason being that when you feel like you cannot breathe, also known as 'Oxygen Debt', right there is when your body works extremely hard to replace the oxygen in your muscles. As a consequence it now increases your metabolic rate and that's when we burn even more calories and our fat. This process releases fatty acids into the bloodstream, which are then metabolised and converted into usable energy.

So, if going to the gym and running 6 kms every single day isn't giving you the weight loss results that you want, then why not practice the things outlined in this book for results that are practical and sustainable?

vibration and frequency of movement

As our society continues to make sociological and spiritual breakthroughs, through things like cultural diversities and personal development, we are now becoming more aware of our spiritual self and open to exploring new ways of viewing who we really are.

The information you are about to read is quite an oversimplified explanation on how our muscles vibrate at a certain frequency and how our environment and our experiences alter the rate at which they vibrate. As you continue to explore and understand yourself through this journey there will come a time where all this new information will all just make sense and will create the most profound shift in how you view yourself and ultimately what you attract in life.

Our existence is something quite remarkable, the more I look into it the more I realise there's so much more we need to know. For example, your body has this innate intelligence where it is continually scanning itself for imperfections and then immediately communicates with the rest of the body as it starts its calibrating process, all in an attempt to keep you as physically able as it possibly can. Its sole purpose is to keep you alive and able to respond to any potential environmental threats, and so that you can continue to hunt and feed yourself.

The Chinese have a word *Ziràn* pronounced as *Zi-Jan*. It's translated as 'Nature' or 'naturally', meaning that which just happens by itself. Your hair grows by itself, your heart beats by itself, your breathing is also autonomous and literally happens by itself, your hormones and glands secrete what they need to by themselves; you don't have voluntary control over these things. We now assume this all happens spontaneously, so what makes them all work? We've previously quoted Nikola Tesla, that the secret of the universe is Energy, Frequency and Vibration. We know a cell's origin is energy and cells are effectively the makeup of who we are. Could it be possible that both the voluntary and involuntary muscles of the body also resonate and vibrate at a certain level of frequency? Could it also be possible that your perceptions and environment affect them?

The human body generates mechanical vibrations at very low frequencies, called infrasonic waves. Infrasonic sound waves are low frequency sound waves that the human ear cannot hear. They are a means of communication for elephants, whales, rhinos, hippos and many other animals. Pigeons use infrasound to infrasound to communicate. By using these lower infrasonic frequencies they're able to communicate hundreds of miles away.

These same low-frequency vibrations are produced by all our biological and physiological processes.

For example, the heart resonance frequency is at 1Hz and the brain has a resonance frequency of 10Hz, everything from our respiratory movements to the blood flow in vessels all resonate at their own frequency. Different organs and muscles of the human body all vibrate at different levels of frequency.

There are three types of infrasonic vibrations. The first type are connected with the heartbeat, muscular contraction and movement. The second with the human respiratory rhythm and the third are called Traube-Hering waves, which reflect the personal states of emotional tension. What's more, is that the rate at which they all vibrate at isn't absolute, as different muscle contractions and stresses increase, then usually so does the frequency and vibration. This shows that the human body is not as simple as we think. According to physics, energy is neither created nor destroyed, but instead changes form. This indicates the potential interaction between you and your environment and how well they either attract or repel each other. The frequency at which your trillions of cells vibrate at is largely affected by your mood, your emotional state and the level of physical activity. From your bicep curl to when you're asleep, everything is energy that vibrates at a certain frequency.

Albert Einstein said that *'Everything is energy and that is all there is to it. Match the frequency of the reality you want and you cannot help get it in reality. There can be no other way. This is not philosophy, This is physics.'* By understanding the basic nature of forces, pressures, and energies through each of these billions of physical events that take place between you and your environment every day and how they affect the rate at which every part of your body vibrates at, will inevitably help to bring your 'BodyMind' back to a state that is in coherence of what you desire to attract in life. If you're now more active and it's improving your personal outlook and physiology all these components are impacting the rate at which your body vibrates at in a positive way.

nutrient assimilation and toxin elimination

Besides being the catalyst for your perfect body and helping you function optimally; movement is also a super important component to the healing process of the body and how your body assimilates nutrients and eliminates toxins. When you're being active around the time of taking in a whole heap of essential micronutrients via your food, or a specific supplement program that you could be on, then the way your body absorbs and processes those micronutrients improves tenfold. That's because movement encourages your body to *assimilate* and utilize *those micronutrients*.

The word assimilate means to include. We must eat whole foods in order to replace the cells that are being damaged in our everyday habits. This becomes very important because in order for you to replace your dying cells you need to be able to assimilate the nutrients you're consuming in order to reap the benefits from those specific nutrients, otherwise you're just wasting your time and inevitably you'll then over stimulate your immune system. This will eventually lead to problems such as chronic fatigue. Whatever is not able to assimilate in the body must now be eliminated through either our urination, perspiration, faeces and respiration, which now brings me to the lymphatic system.

Movement also plays a massive role in allowing the body to process and eliminate toxins from the body. As you begin to take on all the Six Pillars and become a happier and healthier version of yourself the body will begin the healing process and start trading out dead sluggish cells and metabolic waste for all the new vibrant materials it can use to rebuild and repair. Movement now becomes a catalyst to help flush out the bio-toxic waste as your lymphatic system does not have a pump. In our bodies our lymph system is this clear fluid mostly made up of white blood cells that moves through its own network of vessels. The lymph has two jobs: the first is to help deliver nutrients and the second – very importantly – to help clear out toxins as well as recognise any infections and flush them out of the body.

Your lymphatic system also moves free fatty acids throughout the body. It carries the fatty acids to the liver to be processed and metabolised. It's important because our lymphatic system isn't part of our circulatory system and doesn't have its own series of muscles to keep it flowing. It then relies on our movement. So by making movement a staple in your everyday habits it'll improve the way you assimilate nutrients, improve all the functions of the lymphatic system so we can feel better and most important, help get your free fatty acids to the liver to where it can be metabolised and burned so we can get leaner.

As you can see, movement has a myriad of genuine benefits and there is no isolated existence between your body and your mind. We are one great kinetic chain and movement is an integral part of improving your mental, physical, emotional and hormonal health. We are designed to be opportunistic movers and that's just as well, as we're streamlined for the most dynamic movement. Those same movement patterns keep every part of our biology and physiology functioning correctly.

Trivia:
Did you know that you have
4 times more lymph
than blood in the body?

calibrating your body

These static positions are what I personally recommend you start with to improve your energy, mood and mobility. If this is a topic of concern for you, then I recommend you read the book *Pain Free* in order to better understand your pains and apply the right corrective exercises to help calibrate your body. Alternatively you could head to *projectyou.tv* where one of the videos in that program have these exact positions demonstrated. This sequence has been chosen with the intent and focus of lengthening your spine and improving posterior chain, which is a fancy way of saying the back part of your body. The issue is most people all spend most of their time in a closed foetal position which is counter intuitive to your mobility, functionality as well as your energetic flow (bioplasmic body), and so the purpose is to open you up, which immediately improves your posture, your physiology and immediately people around you take your presence a little more seriously. If you don't believe me let's battle test this theory, next time you see a friend, hunch your back into a closed foetal type position, then lower your head slightly and have any conversation with them. See how they respond and if you can try and notice any shift in your energy, as in do you sound convincing, are you taken seriously? Try the same conversation with your chest out standing tall and proud and notice the difference.

Make these a regular practice:

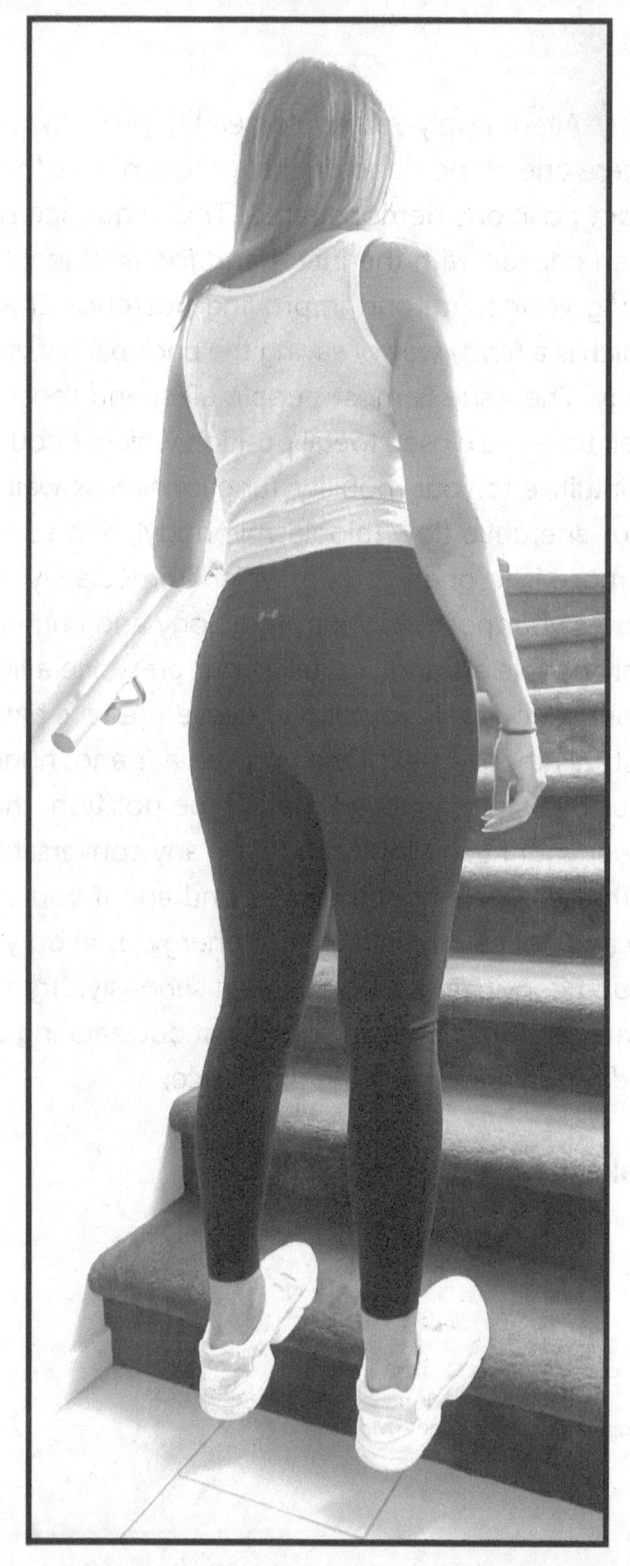

1. GRAVITY DROP

This is by far the easiest one of the lot, quite simply find a step, place the soles of your feet on the edge of the step and quite simply allow your body weight to drop.

I would try and find a set of stairs where you can brace yourself and hold onto a rail of some sort. I would also recommend you wear a good pair of sneakers that have a strong grip.

Once you feel secure, then quite simply breathe into that position and relax there for a total of 3 minutes.

If you feel any sort of discomfort don't be alarmed as it's usually signs of muscles beginning to lengthen themselves again. If that's the case then break it up into 2 or 3 lots of 60 seconds until the 3-minute milestone is achieved.

Please make sure that your feet are straight, and that your feet, ankles and knees are all aligned.

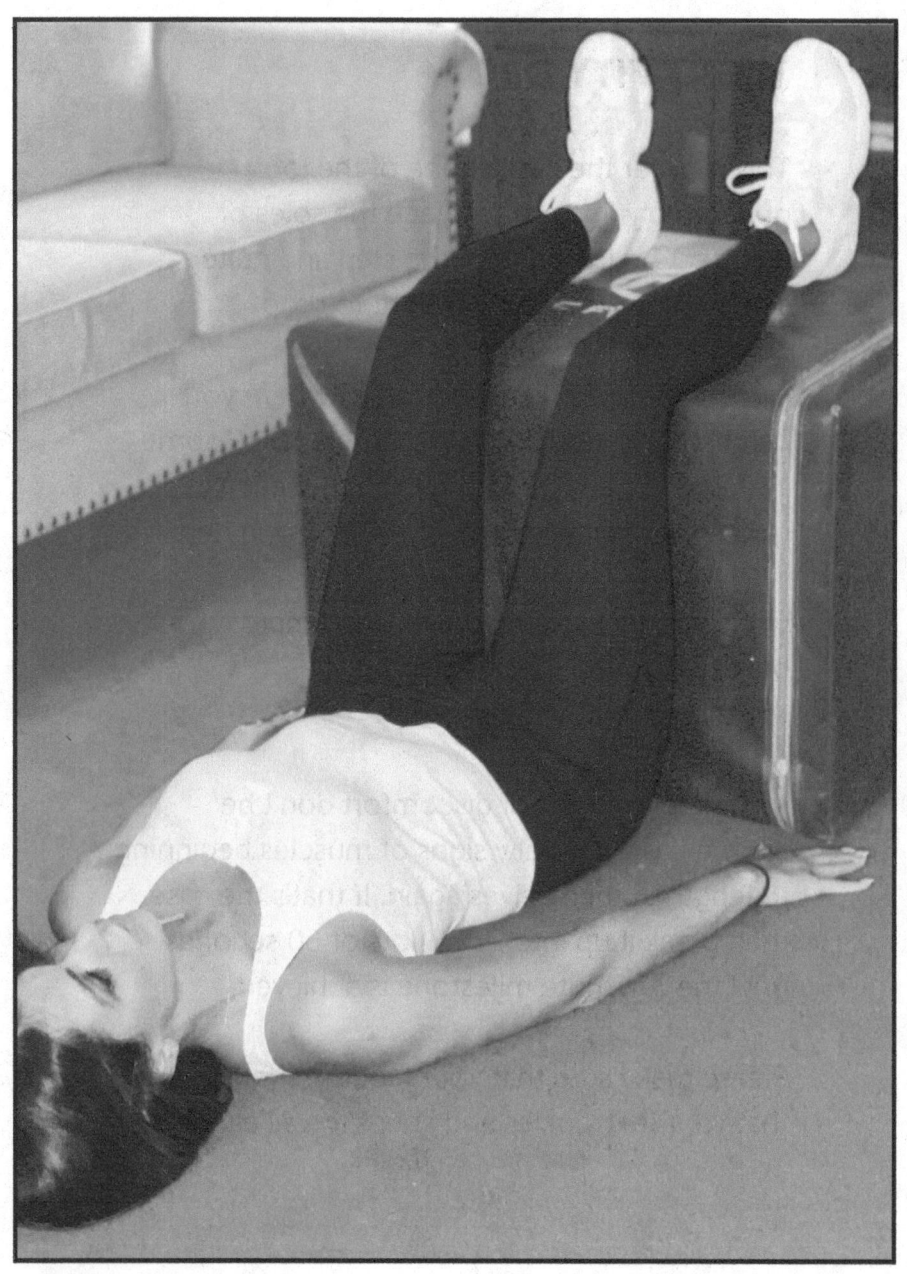

2. STATIC BACK

Lay on your back, with both knees bent at right angles either on a chair, a couch or even a block.

Rest your hands either on your stomach or if you can on the floor with your palms facing up.

Shimmy yourself as close as you can to the object you're placing your legs on and then quite simply allow your back to settle into the floor.

Hold this position for 5 to 10 minutes and focus on your breathing, I personally envisage my femoral head slipping back effortlessly into the acetabulum, which is your hip joint.

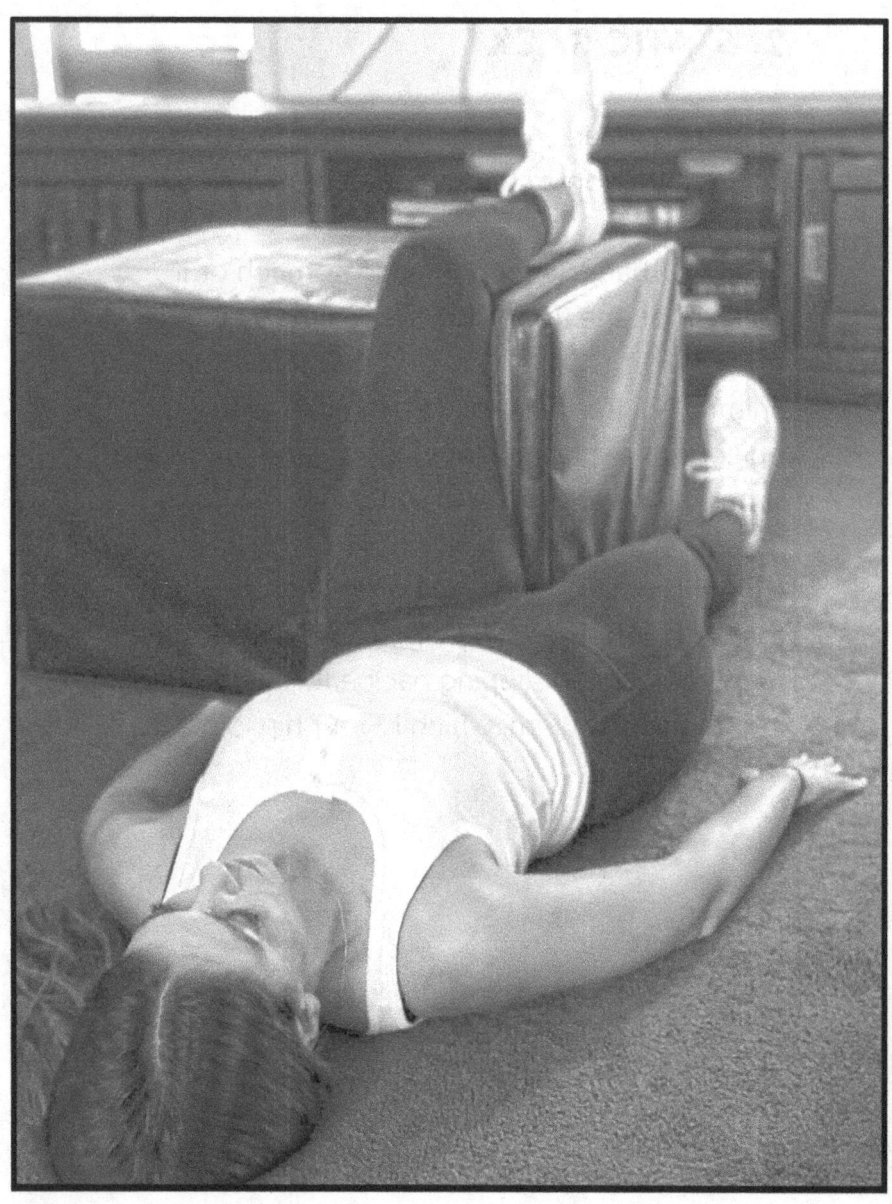

3. SUPINE GROIN STRETCH

Lie on your back with one leg resting on a block or chair, the knee must be bent at a 90-degree angle, whilst the other leg is extended straight out and resting on the floor. (If need be, prop your foot on the extended leg to prevent it from rolling out to the side.)

Hold this position for about 3-5 minutes until the leg is fully relaxed and then repeat on the other side.

If this is done properly then the groin muscles will eventually release the restrictive hold they may have on the leg.

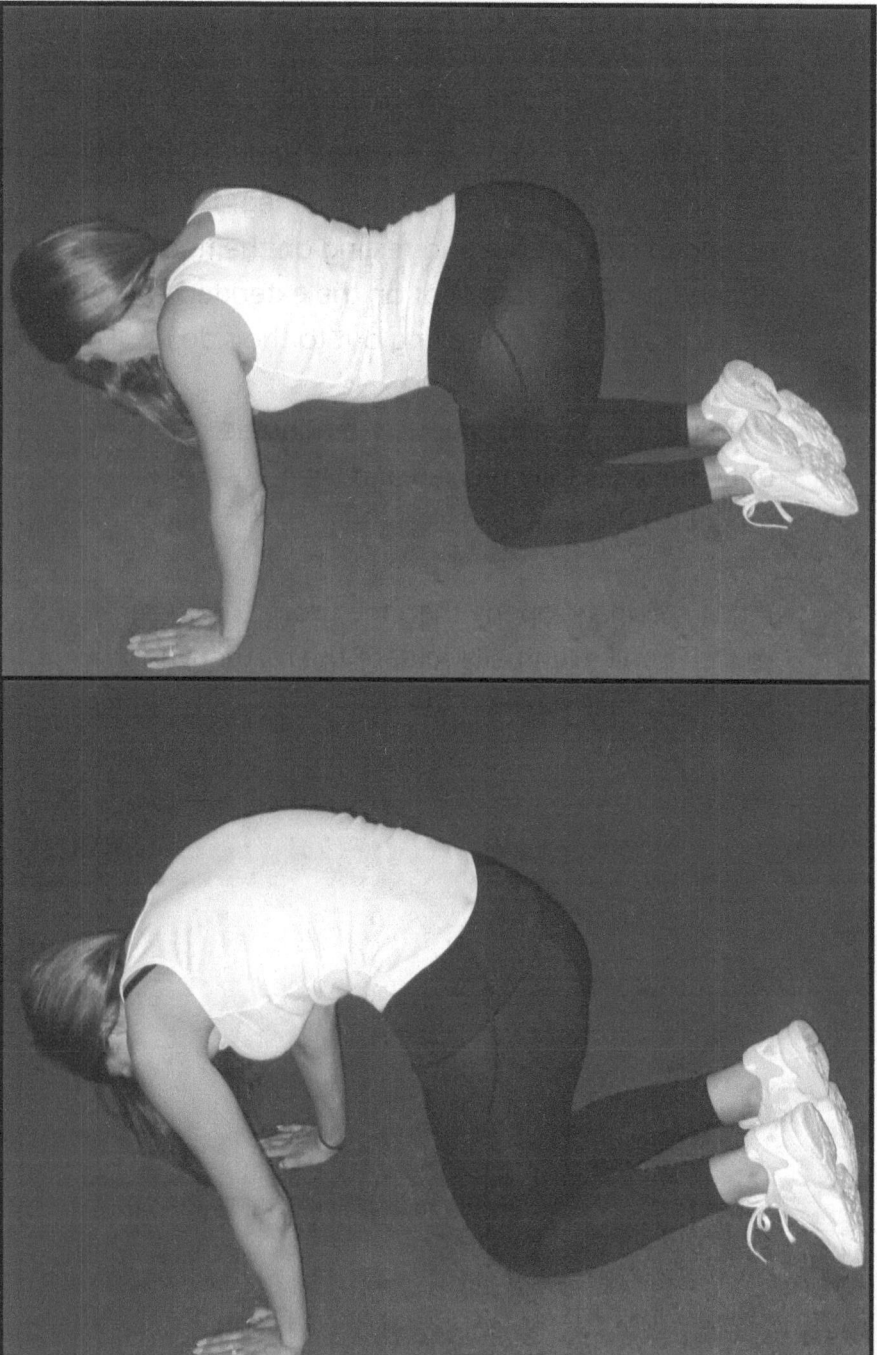

4. CATS & DOGS

This is actually one of my favourite yoga poses as it will help lengthen and stretch your spine.

Starting position is on the floor, on your hands and knees, make sure your knees are aligned with your hips and that your wrists are in alignment with your shoulders.

Now the movement sequence is that you round your back upwards as your head curls to create a curve that runs from your neck to tour buttock, this is what's referred to as the cat pose.

Now slowly allow the back to drop into a position as if you were a horse waiting for someone to jump on your back. As the back has now dropped, raise your head to increase the stretch.

Make sure you breathe into each position, for example inhale in cat and then exhale in dog, make that your sequence for 1 set of ten repetitions.

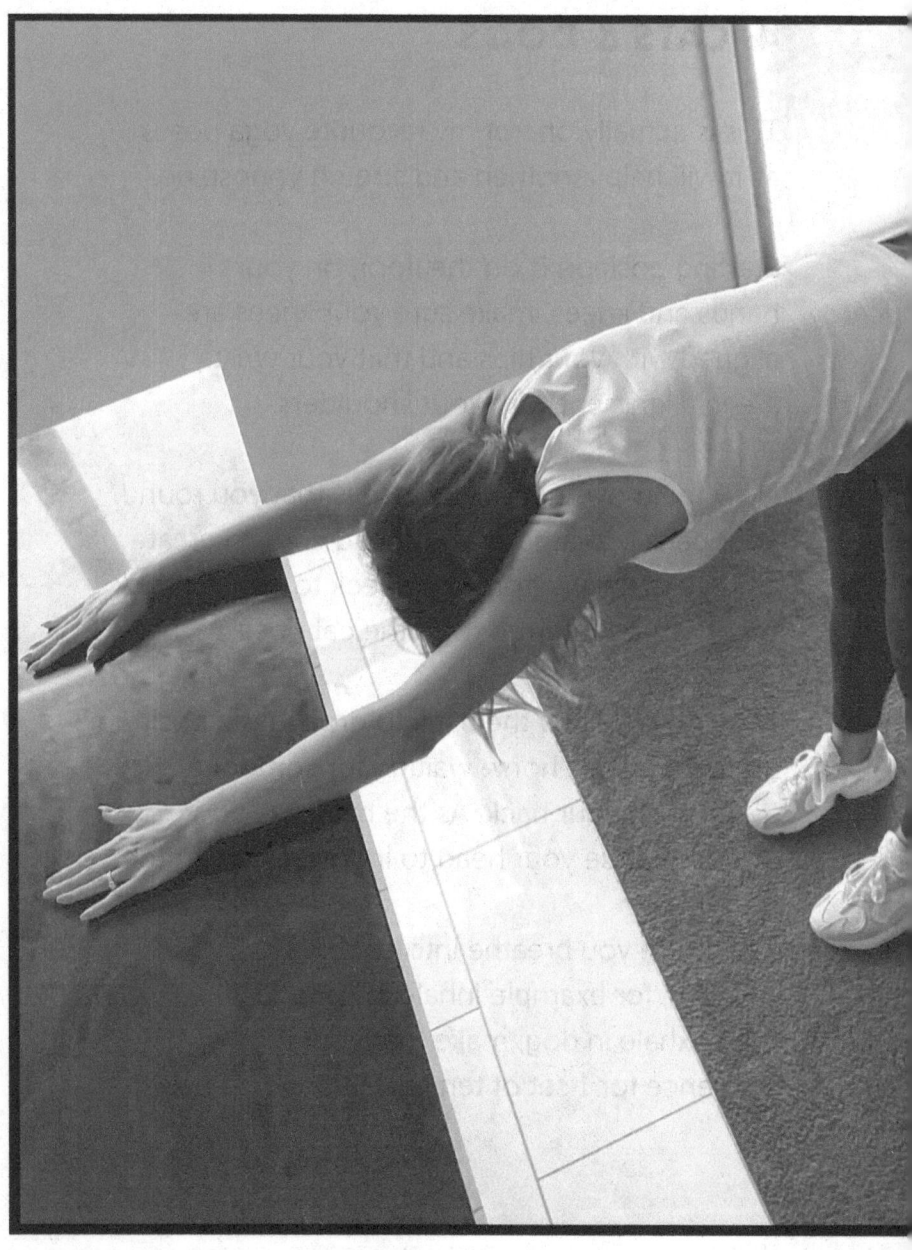

5. COUNTER STRETCH

Place your palms flat on top of a counter or table, I personally use the kitchen bench. However, anything that is about your waist height will do.

Making sure that your feet, ankles, and knees are aligned directly under your hips, bend forward at the hips with your arms stretched out over your head.

Once you've placed your palms flat on the bench then shimmy your feet back until you reach the optimum distance to feel the stretch in your back and initially you may feel it in your hamstrings.

Once you have achieved this then simply allow your head to fall in between your arms and hold that position for 2 minutes.

6. MODIFIED FLOOR BLOCK

Lay on your stomach with your forehead comfortably placed on ground.

Your feet must be pigeon toes, or pointed inwards, and your glutes relaxed.

Once you're able to breathe into the position, you'll notice that your glutes will ease up by themselves, which again highlights that we carry our tension, emotions and stresses in our bodies.

Now place both arms on the blocks so that they are in an elevated position, kind of like when you see a police officer in the movies shout out, 'Freeze!'

And then the person puts their hands up.

Make sure your shoulders are level, as in left to right and then breathe deep into that position and relax for 6 minutes.

7. AIRBENCH

Here is where we add some load to activate all the muscles to help reinforce the latest and newest positioning of the joints. This position is also known as a wall squat.

Make sure that your feet, ankles, knees and hips are in alignment whilst being in the squat position, again breathe into the position and think realignment and activation of these newfound muscles that have been dormant.

The best way I find to get into this position is that I stand with my back flat against the wall. I then begin to walk out slowly whilst dropping the position of my back whilst it remains on the wall until I'm in a squat position and then hold for 3 minutes. For most that may be excessive.

I would suggest you complete sets of 30 seconds with rests in between until you achieve the 3 minutes, and as you progress then increase the duration.

chapter 8:
the second pillar – nutrition

Can you imagine a world where you no longer ever counted calories? And can you imagine a world where you no longer had uncontrollable urges or binges because the diet you chose eliminated everything you loved? Wouldn't it be incredible if you lived in a world where you no longer punished and shamed yourself because you consumed foods you thought were no good for you? The intention of this chapter is to open you up to a new way of thinking and to help you move away from a love/hate relationship with you and food. Our food is meant to have a positive effect on our DNA. However, it's all become so confusing as the media is creating something called the *unconscious bias* where we assume we know it all because we've seen it all, the worse thing is that the media is changing the messaging with nutrition.

Throughout this journey you may have started to notice the pattern that everything we see, feel, breathe and touch is energy that vibrates at a certain frequency that impacts us on a cellular level as well as how we experience our world. It's exactly the same with the food we consume.

I'm forever being asked what I eat. What is your diet like? The truth is I don't go by any sets of rules other than I try and eat organic where possible, free range and wild caught fish. I focus on nutrient dense foods. I can be vegan one day, a carnivore the next and maybe vegetarian on another day. But no matter what I eat it must be full of life and energy.

That's simply because if you eat any type of food that has less energy than your own body then your body will use its own life force to turn that food back into a usable resource. As a result, it leaves you feeling flat and tired, because what you just ate was so dead it sucked the energy right out of you. This is why most people need to drink coffee, eat sweets and stimulants to bring the energy reserves back up.

Another important tip with foods to consume is the *'fresher the better'*. As food decays the nutrients break down. So a general rule of thumb for you to remember is that the longer any food lasts on the shelf the worse off that food is for you. That's one of the reasons why so many people will initially feel amazing on a raw food diet or plant-based diets.

Rather than burden you with responsibility of thinking there's a perfect diet out there, I'd rather liberate you and let you know that there is absolutely no such thing as our requirements changing from day to day and moment to moment, so this is about giving you all the relevant information to be able to make your own choices and never ever have to count another calorie; and even worse, never torment yourself, because you have just had a slice of pizza.

Personally I try and change what I eat from week to week and season to season. As the seasons change, then usually the variety in my diet also changes. One thing that never changes is the quality of the foods I consume must be worthy of putting in my body. Remember the purpose of nutrients are to fuel you, help you repair and recover so that you can continue to function optimally. If your body was a Formula 1 car you wouldn't put cheap fuel in it, you would be searching for the best fuel your money can buy. That should be the exact same mentality when it comes to you and your body.

emotional eating and the bliss point explained

To some degree I'm sure you can relate to the fact that most people have this love/hate relationship with food. So I thought I would shed some light on why most people love the taste of certain foods even though they know that once they're done consuming that extra slice of cake or pizza they'll be left hating themselves and feeling guilty. Yet they can't seem to control the urge to consume these foods. They anticipate the rush they feel during the consumption of these foods in a drug like trance, then loathe themselves in the aftermath of self-disgust and disappointment.

It comes down to two main points, The first is 'emotional eating' and the second is what's referred to as 'the bliss point'. The *food industry* is oversaturated with these processed foods that somehow always seem to hit the sweet spot. Before I explain what the bliss point is, first an interesting fact for you that explains why women are more likely to become *'emotional eaters'* over men. This has largely to do with the hormone 'Oestrogen'. Women naturally have higher levels of oestrogen, and increased levels of oestrogen are known to amplify your ghrelin levels. Ghrelin is the hunger hormone.

As oestrogen amplifies the effects of ghrelin, your ghrelin also begins to intensify the effects on the hippocampus region which is the part of the brain that regulates your motivation, learning, emotions, and memory. This is an over simplified explanation of the process, however, that pattern creates a specific neurological impulse based off both 'Ghrelin and Oestrogen' working on the amygdala, through a region of the brain known as the 'parietal lobe', which is vital for sensory perception and integration, that now allows a heightened amount of neural transfer of neurotransmitters and electrical connective energy to flow faster kind of like a rush of energy, which in short, means you get addicted.

The 'bliss point' where scientists run extensive tests to find the perfect balance of sugar, fat and salt for any food processing company. For example, a McDonalds Big Mac will give us a massive dopamine response from the reward centre in the brain. So the pattern now becomes see food, eat food, feel good, repeat and time after time that will program that pattern or 'Addiction' deep in the subconscious.

When you're eating sugar your body sends a signal to the brain that says, 'Remember what you're eating and where you found it!' This lays the foundation for the See Food, Eat Food, Feel Good, Repeat. Also referred to as trigger, behaviour, reward!

Great news is that *addictions* are learned behaviours and so to help you break the trancelike cycle and give you time to remain composed, I'd suggest you become aware of all your bodily sensations, so that every time you find yourself questioning why you feel the urge to have certain foods you don't necessarily want, shift your awareness and attention to your stomach. Take five small sips of water and then when you're calm ask yourself, 'Am I genuinely hungry right now? How hungry am I? What am I actually hungry for?' By doing so you'll break that initial reflex of just indulging in that chocolate or donut whilst torturing yourself in the process.

A cool hack to help you overcome the memories of certain foods created by the bliss point is to stay clear of the foods that you are addicted to for a period of about two weeks. Simply because the tongue only remembers the taste of food for up to 10 days, so all you really need to do to detox your taste buds is remain abstinent from that food for a couple of weeks and when you go back to eating it, it will never taste quite as good as you remembered it last.

frequency food

Why different people can have different responses to the same foods precisely comes down to the fact that we are all made of energy, and we therefore require the consumption of energy in the form of food, air and water for sustenance and good health. The ancient Greeks introduced the world to the concept of energy and its effects on humans, animals, plants and our health. We are all connected spiritually by energy. Aristotle said that *'we are all one, love is the cause of unity of all things.'*

When eating fresh organic fruits and vegetables off the tree the vibrational energy benefit of the food is high and rich in nutrients from the sun. Most fast-food restaurants, large grocery food chains offer food that is of a *very low energy* vibrational quality, thus not adding any valuable nutrients to the body. Foods that are prepared lovingly and peacefully have a significantly more positive effect on our cells and how they function. Let's assume that you're like everyone else and you have had this habitual dialogue and belief system that certain foods, for example pizza, is bad for you. That belief will keep the foods you assume that are bad for you from being good for you, and that's because your beliefs have a massive input into how the food is received by the cells.

Eat for the feeling of vitality, eat for fuel, eat for the benefit and pleasure of the food rather than the result of it. That's when you'll start noticing what foods you begin to gravitate towards and in time you'll develop the skills to understand what your body needs as you start to listen to yourself. What you'll find is that what you gravitate towards on that day will be completely compatible to how you're feeling and what you need. For example there was a day I wasn't feeling well and went to the supermarket to buy some food and started craving the weirdest thing in particular, *'Eggplant Skin'*. Unsure why, I started researching the benefits and found that that's exactly what I needed to feel better. Your dietary intake is not only responsible for giving you the energy to get through the day, it also has the ability to improve your consciousness, as in your spiritual elevation, can help keep your mind sharp, as well as improve your physical fitness and hormonal health. Even the way the food is prepared has a direct effect on the energy and frequency of that food. Every single bioactivity performed in the body is only made possible by the cells in the body; and those cells are made up of the foods we consume and is the main reason why I am so selective in what food and water I consume.

Higher Frequency Foods:
Fresh certified organic fruit and vegetables, living grains such as sprouts, herbal teas, herbs and spices, pure or specialised filtered water, for example, reverse osmosis. Healthy oils such as olive oil and coconut oil. Eating raw food, dehydrated and lightly steamed foods, anything uncooked, minimally processed raw, organic and activated nuts and seeds, fermented foods, raw chocolate, raw honey and maple syrup.

Lower Frequency Foods:
Genetically modified foods (GMO), all foods that have been treated with chemicals and pesticides, herbicides, rodenticides, anything pasteurised such as milk, cheese or yoghurt or bleached foods such as white rice and flour, sugars. Artificial sweeteners,

soft drinks, processed meats, fish and poultry that are packaged and canned. Unhealthy oils such as canola and cottonseed oils, margarine, and vegetable oils, frozen pre-made foods, foods cooked or heated in a microwave and the most notorious of the lot, 'Fast Foods'.

the no diet diet

No one can really determine how many calories are needed to be consumed every day for you to reduce your weight, and the reason is quite simple. Your caloric needs *will* vary from day to day, season to season and that's only the start.

Biochemist Rodger William published a book called *Biochemical Individuality*, where he highlighted in detail the anatomical variations within us; how our size, our shape and even our location can have an impact on our metabolic rate. Even the way we function both intrinsically and extrinsically can have an effect on our nutritional and metabolic needs.

Another important study in validating how caloric needs will change as climate and food staples change in each of the demographics of people and race. The book *'Nutrition and Physical Degeneration'* was written in the early 1930s and focussed on the health and the diet of native people, also comparing the health of natives who have deviated from their natural diets.

For example, the Inuit staple diet is high in fats and protein, compared to the diet of South American natives, who ate a staple diet of predominantly plant-based foods.

Throughout the research process of acquiring this information the author *Weston A Price* never saw any malignant disease amongst the Inuit and the South American natives over the 36 years of his extensive research. Price's research also goes against the current belief system of many supposed nutrition gurus that preach the negative impact high meat diets have on our health. I do have to say that if current belief on eating meats was based on the lack of quality of these mass-produced meats that the general population is consuming, then I would have to agree that they are bad for you. I personally am a massive advocate of quality organic free-range produce. I need to consume less to get that same amount of nutrients essential for my overall health and wellbeing.

One of the most profound nutritional books I have read, *Metabolic Type Diet*, emphasises the importance of eating balanced meals. This means something different for everyone. We really should be focussing on the diet that our individual systems are designed to eat. These differences depend on many factors such as place of origin, genetics, diet or diets while growing up and diets and health issues during adulthood.

calories in vs. calories out

What does that even mean?

'To lose weight, simply burn more calories than you consume.' This has been glamorised, but it doesn't explain everything. It's easy to back this claim by appealing to the first law of thermodynamics. But what's often overlooked is that the first law of thermodynamics takes place in a closed system. In what is called 'thermal equilibrium', energy can neither be created, nor destroyed. Energy is conserved. The key here is that if a system gets more mass it's because it has taken in more energy than it being given out on that beach or that there might be some family event with jumping castles and rides on the beach. Or it could even be that the police aren't letting anyone leave the car park until the event is finished. These are all reasons why the car park is overfilled and crowded with energy.

It's the same thing with obesity. If you're saying that people get fat because they consume more energy than they expend, that is the obvious answer, but it in no way states anything about why that person is obese. This theory was embraced in the 1950s and became the conventional wisdom. No one really questioned it as it seemed obvious. However, the laws of thermodynamics say absolutely nothing about obesity.

If we were to use any one of the laws of thermodynamics, the one that gets overlooked and is closer to explaining this is the second law, which is also the law of common sense where it states, 'Energy will be lost and energy will be used up in making available energy', which needs to be taken into account.

ɔ the oversimplified calories in versus calories 't theory has been glamorised without any real

project YOU

expends, and if the system decreases in mass then the system is expending more energy than it takes in. Energy can't be created from nothing and it can't disappear either. That's because energy can only change forms.

The issue is that this law says absolutely nothing about why it's happening, and the human body is not a closed system, nor is it in thermal equilibrium, as we expel heat all day, we urinate, we sweat. The law is merely an association, it is always true but it tells us absolutely nothing about the person or the reasons why this person is gaining mass.

Here's an example to help you understand what I mean. Let's say you were driving to the beach on a hot day and you go to park in the only car park there is and completely filled with cars. Call this 'energy'. You ask the car park management why there are so many cars ('energy') in this parking lot. Th' is like asking why a person is carrying more fa' their body than another person. Car park ma ment now says it's because more people ? ing in then going out, which is the obvic But that doesn't address the reason park is overfilled with energy. The re cess energy could be that there's biochemistry taken into consideration or no real knowledge of what's happening intrinsically. For example, how different foods are used up in the body, or what metabolic advantage you could have by eating certain foods while avoiding others.

Understanding this component makes all the difference in creating sustainable change. Counting calories isn't the way and if you starve yourself in an attempt to lose weight you will give your metabolism the biggest reason to slow down and maybe even shut down your reproductive system; and weaken your immune system as well as create other hormonal imbalances.

types of diets

In traditional fashion this book isn't a dictation of what to do but rather an eye-opening journey designed to empower you with knowledge to make better choices to a more practical, sustainable and healthier you. Embracing the tools and information that have been delicately selected in this book will prove to be one of the most powerful and transformational things you could do in your life. So instead of just telling you what to eat, how about I explain the different diet types and you try them all for yourself and see what suits you the most? The idea is that you now never have to follow any fads but rather listen to the needs and requirements of your body. As I explained earlier, if I feel like vegetables then usually that's my body's way of telling me I need them and so I find myself eating differently every day, week or month.

For example if I now eat a banana and it's the best tasting banana I've ever had that's a sign my body needs all the benefits associated with that banana. But then say a week later I don't find that banana is as tasty, or that I'm not craving it, then that is a sign that I more than likely don't need it as much. I encourage you to pay attention to your body and what it tells you. It may take some practice but eventually you'll work it out and the more you listen the better you'll feel.

paleo

The Paleo diet has become one of the fastest growing dietary concepts and the idea behind it is that the key to improving your long-term health is to abandon the modern agricultural type diets and to readopt the diet of the Palaeolithic period, which is basically the *'stone age era'*. The concept was based on taking information that we knew about the past and by adapting it, we can help can combat some health issues we face today. The key to understanding this diet is done through comparing pre-agricultural societies or hunter-gatherer societies to societies based on modernised and mechanised agriculture. If we can emulate the diet of our ancestors, it might just improve the longevity of our health and lives.

Our Palaeolithic ancestors ate what they were able to hunt or gather – whole, unprocessed foods that were predominantly meat based, but supplemented with vegetables, fruits, nuts and oils.

Palaeolithic diets excluded grains, legumes and dairy which if I'm completely honest isn't such a bad concept. However, there are obvious differences between the Palaeolithic era and modern day in humans and how we've evolved. But I'm not here to sway your opinion just simply introduce you to some dietary concepts and pray it helps you work out what suits you, your lifestyle and requirements.

There are a number of foods that are considered okay as part of building a healthy Paleo diet. These foods are nutrient rich and are considered to be the cornerstone of maintaining healthy metabolic, digestive and immune systems. However, Paleo doesn't allow for too much variety so if you're looking to have more balance and variety in your diet then this diet may not be practical for you, the main components of this diet are:

Grass-fed meats and preferably organic, which I'm a massive fan of as they contain more nutrients such as antioxidants, conjugated linoleic acid (CLA), omega-3 and vitamins than grain-fed and mass-produced meats.

Seafood, which is high in vitamins and minerals, including zinc and potassium. Seafood is also low in fat (average of less than 2% fat) and high in protein and more importantly rich in omega-3 fatty acids.

Eggs, preferably organic, which are an exceptional source of complete protein and rich in nutrients. A single egg contains Vitamin A, Vitamins B5, B12 and B2 as well as Calcium and Zinc.

Fruits and vegetables are rich in antioxidants, vitamins, minerals and phytonutrients that protect us from all sorts of diseases.

Nuts, seeds, healthy fats and oils. Walnut oil is a great source of omega 3 acids and high in antioxidants including ellagic acid. Extra virgin olive oil can control cholesterol levels and is linked closely with good heart health. Coconut oil consists of medium chain triglycerides (MCTs). MCTs are easy to digest and are a great immediate fuel source and one of my favourites. Avocado oil has a high concentration of vitamin E and chlorophyll.

veganism

Veganism is a non-violent practice and lifestyle that is predominantly concerned about the environment and animal rights. I wouldn't call this a diet, but more so a movement and a lifestyle choice.

Veganism is a plant-based diet and has become a massive new craze. The two main reasons why I think people adopt a vegan diet: the first is for the environment and the second is animal rights. The majority of people who adopt veganism start to feel better and see instant benefits. That's because they're now having nutrient dense foods that are full of life and moving away from all the processed sugar loaded foods.

Some of the positives to a vegan diet is that there's been some evidence that shows that it can help or better assist to protect your bones and bone density as well as improve heart health and lower the risk of cancer. Besides adopting a plant-based diet and lifestyle, vegans are also opposed to the psychological and physical stress that animals may endure as a result of modern farming practices. In short veganism is a lifestyle that excludes all animal products and attempts to limit the exploitation of animals.

A vegan diet involves eating only food products made from plants and avoiding animal products. There are however a couple of concerns I personally have in respects to only having a plant-based diet. Genetics and genetic differences play a massive role in how well we are able to convert precursor nutrients into the nutrients we actually need and assimilate. For example, Omega 3 fatty acids, EPA and DHA, which are long chain omega 3 fats that have been shown to improve brain function and cardiovascular function. Primarily we get those from eating oily type fish. There are no sources of the Omega 3 fats in a plant-based diet, except for algae. However, you can have walnuts which contain alpha linoleic acid. To some degree we can convert some of this plant-based omega 3 fat into the longer chain EPA and DHA fat. The only thing is such a small amount gets converted into EPA and DHA and so at times you may struggle getting so much flaxseed oil and nuts into your diet on a day-to-day basis.

So if this is the type of diet that is resonating with you then I would strongly suggest that you supplement with micro-algae, because it has pre-formed DHA Omega 3 fats in it so you bypass the whole conversion issue. The second point is the deficiency in Vitamin B12, even though things like seaweed, spirulina and nutritional yeast are said to contain B12 they're not the cleanest source of Vitamin B12. A Vitamin B12 supplement would definitely be something you'd need to invest in as studies show that 83 percent of vegans are deficient in Vitamin B12. Another important point is that we also need amino acids. They are divided into two main groups and that's essential and non-essential amino acids. The essential meaning the body does not and cannot produce them. The body must source them via your nutrition. Animal based protein has the complete spectrum of all 9 essential amino acids, yet the plant-based protein doesn't always have a complete spectrum of all 9 essential amino acids.

And so although you have the right to choose whatever diet you prefer to adapt, my role is only to highlight the facts. From them you are free to make up your mind. You can do additional research if you like, too. If you decide to adopt the veganism concept then you must know exactly what you're doing in order to have a healthy vegan diet. Just because you're eating plant-based foods doesn't mean that it's completely healthy for your bodily requirements. If your ethical preference is to have a vegan diet then you'll need to have a perfect vegan diet for it to be healthy. You'll need to know what you're doing with supplementation in order to get the nutrient needs that aren't being met through the diet.

vegetarianism

Vegetarianism, much like its counterpart veganism is predominantly a plant-based diet. However, the core difference is that whilst vegetarians do not eat meat they still may consume animal-based products like dairy and eggs. Much like veganism, a person does not have to eat meat to get all the nutrients they need for good health. However, it's always encouraged to research the foods you're consuming and to supplement with any nutrients your diet or meal plan is deficient in, in order to maintain optimal health.

Again anyone who chooses to follow a vegetarian diet tends to consume a high proportion of fresh, healthful, plant-based foods, which provide antioxidants and fibre. As a result, they immediately feel the benefits and tend to become more active in making overall healthy choices.

Many studies agree that a vegetarian diet can offer a range of health benefits. Studies show that a vegan or vegetarian diet may reduce the risk of cardiovascular disease and various types of cancer. A plant-based diet can provide a wide variety of healthy, nutritious foods. However, did you know that fruits and vegetables are also rich in phytonutrients? These chemicals evolved in plants to help protect them from environmental threats such as ultraviolet radiation and plant-eating parasites. Those same plant protectors do the same for us. The four key features of phytonutrients are that they have immune system boosting properties, they have extremely potent anti-inflammatory properties, they are rich in antioxidants and they act as a cleanser and detoxifier.

The phytonutrients that are associated with the colours of both fruits and vegetables are as follows. Green fruits and vegetables are rich in lutein, red fruits and vegetables are rich in lycopene, orange and yellow are rich in beta-carotene, blue and purple provide you with a rich source of resveratrol, and white is rich in allicin.

ketogenic diet

The ketogenic diet is often conflated with the Paleo diet. Paleo still allows carbohydrates from groups of whole foods such as fruits, vegetables and unrefined sweeteners. Whereas the keto diet restricts certain sources of carbohydrates, including starchy vegetables, most fruits, grains, sweeteners and most legumes. The Keto diet is a high fat and extremely low carbohydrate diet, with the intent being that by using high fats as your primary source of energy it forces your body to use different energy pathways, by that I mean that our bodies have this alternative pathway to using or creating bioavailable energy in times of emergency which are known as ketone bodies.

These ketone bodies are produced in order to keep you functioning optimally. They are used instead of glucose to fuel your brain and your tissue. They're also known to have a very strong anti-inflammatory effect; they've also been prescribed by physicians to anyone who suffers from seizures. When you are on a ketogenic diet your body is in a state that nutritionists have dubbed 'ketosis'.

On a ketogenic diet there's some great data that supports people losing a significant amount of body fat in the short term. My only reservation is this diet is a very restrictive diet for most people and may not be sustainable for them in the long term, especially as there are drawbacks like the ketogenic flu. As you transition between carbohydrates being your primary fuel source to fats now being your primary fuel source, you can have flu-like symptoms but you don't actually have the flu! The analogy I'll use here is that if you are as old as myself most people used to run gas and petrol to save on fuel costs and there was either a button or a switch that would change the car's running fuel source from gas to petrol or vice versa. When you flipped the switch as the car was changing its fuel source it would start to run very rough until the new fuel source had taken over so we would experience some shaking as though the car was about to stall, which was only temporary.

There are different degrees of being in ketosis and that often due to the amount of fat, protein and carbohydrate ratio or percentage. The fastest way of getting into a state of ketosis and sustaining it is by consuming 70% healthy fats, 25% protein and only 5% carbohydrates in the form of non-starchy vegetables.

This may be a difficult program to get your head around as most people have been convinced to steer clear of fats. It has been argued since at least the mid-20th century in Western countries that fat is bad for us. The fact is that fats are calorie dense with 9 calories per gram of fat compared to carbohydrates, which have only 4 calories per gram. Now keep in mind that not all calories are alike and in my opinion, fats are a more efficient source of fuel. Again the idea with this diet is that we condition the body to run on fats, therefore you're effectively getting more energy per gram. In return you'll find that you actually get away with eating less and feel satiated for longer.

If this is a diet you'd like to try then remember this ratio will give you the truest form of a ketogenic diet:

**70% Fat,
25% Protein
and 5% Carbohydrates**

Acceptable Fats on this Diet:
Saturated fats: lard, tallow, chicken fat, duck fat, goose fat, clarified butter/ghee, butter, and coconut oil. Monounsaturated: avocado, macadamia, and olive oil. Polyunsaturated: omega 3s especially from animal sources, fatty fish like salmon and seafood, organic egg yolk, natural and raw nuts, in particular if you can consume activated nuts.

Acceptable Protein on this Diet:
Grass-fed meat: beef, lamb, goat, venison, wild-caught fish and seafood, free range pork and poultry, eggs, ghee, butter – these are high in healthy omega 3 fatty acids (avoid sausages and meat covered in breadcrumbs, hot dogs, or any meat that is processed) offal, grass-fed: liver, heart, kidneys and other organ meats.

Acceptable Carbohydrates for this Diet:
Leafy greens: bok choy, spinach, lettuce, chard, chives, endive, radicchio, some cruciferous vegetables like kale (dark leaf), kohlrabi, radishes, celery stalk, asparagus, cucumber, summer squash, zucchini, spaghetti squash, bamboo shoots and sprouts.

intermittent fasting

Intermittent fasting is an eating pattern where you cycle between periods of eating and fasting. Human fasting is far from a new concept. It's something our bodies do every time when we're asleep. Fasting has also been used as part of religious practices since ancient times. Intermittent fasting carries this time period of not eating further into the day. One misconception that most people have about intermittent fasting is that they assume they're starving themselves. That's far from the truth, when you enter a fasting state it then gives your body the green light to now go on and use its stored nutrients and stored energy forms to keep you functioning optimally.

There are many forms of intermittent fasting and the one I personally love is the 16 - 8 circadian fast, when I nominate an 8-hour window to consume all the whole foods I need to consume, and then fast for 16 hours. The deal that I personally make with my body is that I will nourish you for the next 8 hours with nutrient rich whole foods and then I will get out of your way, body, and allow you to work your magic for me, and keep my hormones in check, allowing me to look and feel amazing.

By cutting back on the amount of time your body is processing food, your hormones will regulate more easily, as well as balance your insulin sensitivity, which is the hormone that signals the body to store fat. Intermittent fasting can be challenging, however extremely rewarding, because it calls for some fasting discipline throughout the day. If you find that to be the case for you then I would suggest you pick an 8-hour window that allows the hardest part to be done whilst you're sleeping.

When you're fasting you increase your body's resistance to toxins, due to the fact that your body goes into a protective state to ensure you're still able to function optimally. In return it will now improve your overall functionality, and more importantly slow down your cell ageing process.

Another reason I absolutely love intermittent fasting is because it allows the body to now work for you as it was meant to. The body is designed to respond to any stimulus that comes at it, and intermittent fasting is a form of acute stress stimuli. It's kind of like exercise. When you stress your body after exercising you get the benefits of improved cognitive function, benefits of weight loss, etc.

Equally, when you expose your body to intermittent fasting you'll find an improved mental sharpness and weight loss. Also, you'll get an increase in growth hormone production whilst improving insulin sensitivity. Insulin is a hormone that instructs your body to store energy in addition to regulating blood sugar levels. Higher insulin levels equals more fat storage. Improving your insulin sensitivity will allow you to absorb more of the nutrients from the foods you consume.

Intermittent fasting also helps with a reduction of inflammation as well as an increased percentage of a process known as autophagy, which is the process of the removal of cellular waste. It increases the effectiveness of this process by up to 300%. Autophagy comes from the Greek word meaning 'Self Eating', whereby the cells are now recycling damaged cell parts.

It's a bit like when you take the garbage out. Every cell has its own garbage disposal called the lysosome, an organelle which is sent to the liver to be used as energy or recycled into new cells. This system also allows for an increased production of neurotrophic factors, which help protect your brain. There's an increase in the production of Human Growth Hormone, which will help you look and feel younger. Having more of this hormone tends to mean you're feeling younger, more vibrant and most importantly more energetic. Lastly, intermittent fasting will help **improve leptin and ghrelin sensitivity**: Ghrelin is known as the hunger hormone and is effectively what tells the body you need to eat, whilst leptin is a hormone that is released by your fat cells and is what tells the body that you either need to burn fat or store more fat. Intermittent fasting can help balance out these two hormones and improve overall functionality.

Trivia:
'There have been studies that link fasting or being in a fasted state to increased blood flow in the abdominal region, which results in a more effective, abdominal fat loss.'

---

chapter 9:
the third pillar – breathing

What if there was an exercise that could change the pH of your blood, that could make it either more acidic or alkaline within a minute? What if that same exercise could boost your digestion and improve your health? Breathing may not be as simple as you think and before we delve into the depths of the myriad of benefits around breathing, here's a small quote by Rumi. *'With life as short as a half-taken breath, don't plant anything but love.'* Even though the quote's intention and this chapter's intention aren't in complete alignment, I wanted to use that quote to highlight two main points. Humans tend to breathe shallow breaths and take in half as much oxygen as we could be getting, simply because we don't breathe properly. Second, life is too short to worry about hatred and the past and it's time to start planting more love in your life so that you future bears the fruits of happiness, love, joy and abundance.

We live in a world of information, whereby ignorance is only a choice. This exercise should come naturally to us, yet it's something most struggle with unconsciously. Breathing properly can help control your nervous system and your endocrine system. Equally, if we don't breathe properly it will cause havoc on the body. Breathing is part of the autonomic nervous system. The basics of breathing is a topic that is usually overlooked and although the impact may seem subtle, the benefits are certainly profound in improving your mental, physical and emotional health. The issue is that due to lifestyle choices, the way we've adapted as a race is rendering us unable to connect with our evolutionary primitive programming and in particular the way we were designed to breathe and both alkaline and oxygenate our cells. Most people do not know how to breathe and as a result we actually need to re-educate ourselves. If you breathe as though a baby does, then you're doing it well. However, chances are you're not. Right now you're probably thinking *of course I am breathing*, but my question to you is 'are you breathing properly?'

Here are some reasons for you to start breathing properly. Without breathing we will die quite quickly. Three minutes without oxygen or air, your brain will be in trouble. You can survive without food or water for a lot longer than three minutes. The point I make is that we can do quite well without most things, but we cannot do well, for long, without breathing.

All of our physiological systems are dependent upon breathing for life. If we are not getting enough oxygen into our lungs it triggers an alarm reaction. Even how we breathe influences our blood-gas ratio (oxygen to carbon dioxide). If we breathe too fast, or hyperventilate, and get too much oxygen, that will stimulate the fight or flight reaction (sympathetic nervous system) and the leading contributor to anxiety.

Conversely, if we also breathe too slowly, we can also trigger a fight or flight reaction because we are not getting enough oxygen. A lot of people will hold their breath when they react to stress. Breathing pattern disorders can cause common problems such as muscle spasms, digestive troubles, sleeping disorders, cognitive dysfunctions and neurological symptoms, just to name a few.

Breathing is very important to maintain your pH levels (the acidity/alkalinity) in the body. If you're not breathing properly then the amount of oxygen in your blood and cells would be reduced significantly, rendering you to be at risk of being in an acidic state. Either way, whether overly alkaline or overly acidic, both of which will cause problems in the body. A key problem for people is the consumption of processed foods – for example, white sugar.

White sugar can acidify the blood quite quickly so as a defence mechanism we unconsciously start to hyperventilate to produce an alkalising effect on the blood. I make reference to this because it is almost impossible to correct a person's breathing disorder if there is too much sugar in their diet. So, if you're genuinely wanting to improve your breathing and health, you need to start with reducing the amount of simple or refined carbohydrates you consume such as soft drinks, lollies, chocolate, and sugars. All these so-called 'tasty treats' use additives to replace fat in an attempt to make them palatable.

Breathing is important to our physiology. Breathing properly has a huge effect on our psychology. 'Faulty breathing' is linked to a large number of health problems, costing people and society millions of dollars daily because of lost time, productivity and costly medical bills.

breatharianism

To most of us breathing is something we do to live and overlook its importance and significance, kind of like when we look at the sky and don't even notice the blue, it just is and breathing happens by itself. All of the Six Pillars are extremely important in creating the most complete and comprehensive *'life changing spectrum'* in your quest of improving your mental, physical and emotional health, again even though the changes may be subtle the impacts are profound. Every time you trace any of the Six Pillars back to their origin and source, you will see that they all originate in the universal and unified field of energy both scientifically and spiritually. The significance in this illustration is that we shouldn't be so quick to overlook anything we are gifted in life with, in particular the air we breathe.

There is a group of people called *'Breatharians'* who are practitioners of pranic yoga, which is a union between physical activities as well as spiritual practices. They live off the energy their breath and the sun provides them with. Nikola Tesla wrote an article in support of breatharian living called 'Talking With the Planets', where he states that 'why should a living being not be able to obtain all the energy it needs for the performance of its life functions from the environment, instead of through consumption of food, and transforming, by a complicated process, the energy of chemical combinations into life sustaining energy?'

What I gather is that his intended message in this article is that why shouldn't a person be able to cultivate energy and nourish the cells of the body from the sun and breath, as the make-up of who we are is energy that vibrates at a certain frequency. Our eyes, our muscles, all of our vital organs are all energy that vibrates at their relevant frequency and that if the sun's energy and atmospheric energy all originate from the same source then why waste time having to break down food into energy when you can get it directly from your environment? I personally would never attempt to become a breatharian, but found this practice fascinating and very relevant in highlighting the significance of improving your life force by simply improving the way you breathe.

Breatharians believe everything a human body needs to survive is contained in the energy that surrounds the body itself, their belief is that they can live off the pranic energy of light and air, kind of like how a plant derives its energy from the sun. According to yogic philosophies there are different levels of *prana energy*, however, you genuinely need to be physically, mentally and spiritually evolved before you can be aware of it and allow the body to absorb it. By applying things like visualisation in their meditation, coupled with belief, focus and intent, in a process known as Sun Gazing, breatharians progressively learn how to feel and absorb the energy from the sunlight and nourish their bodies. They believe that by using your eyes as a photosynthesising organ that you can get all the nourishment needed directly from the sun and your surrounding atmosphere. This may seem farfetched, however, in the typical nature of creating the content of this book I again embarked on a research frenzy where I found a plethora of scientific experiments highlighting that there is *'electron density'* in the atmosphere and that the density varies in each of its layers. In ancient Vedic texts it is said that this electron density has the capability to heal the body from anything, seeing them sing a mantra to Suryanarayana, the God of the sun, every morning. The ancient Greeks used the sunlight as a method for healing the body with what was known as heliotherapy where patients were placed in sunbeds for most of the day and were able to heal from almost all diseases. As recently as several decades ago in Rome, they had sunlight rooms in their hospitals, which were known to accelerate healing from wounds and diseases.

Besides the energy from the Sun, Breatharians also live off Prana, which is a Sanskrit word that translates as *'Life Air'* or *'Life force'*. Prana is defined as an energy that runs through the entire universe and connects all of creation, and that this universal energy is all the human body needs to survive, which is now inhaled through breath and absorbed via sunlight. Prana is an *intelligent energy* as it will function differently in each individual person which is largely dependent on their level of spiritual mastery and personal development. Practitioners of this school of thought believe that when you're able to achieve complete balance between your physical and spiritual self, then you will have absolutely no physical ailments, no matter what variables you face in life or what emotional frequencies you're vibrating at, as long as you're in tune with your prana/chi/energy and take control of it then you will inevitably have mental, physical and emotional balance at all times.

I bet you're wondering how this is possible and that surely this is just some sort of spiritual conspiracy and extremism and that there isn't real scientific evidence to support these claims?

If so, then let's look into the science behind these claims, *'Solar Energy' (Sun Prana)* is energy from sunlight and light is scientifically known to be a wave of both *'electric and magnetic fields'*. For breatharians the Solar Prana integrates with the body promoting the most amazing health, whereas science believes that the *'Air Energy' (Air prana)* that is absorbed by the lungs through breathing is distributed through the energy centres of our *'BioPlasmic'* body, which is a fancy scientific label that claims that the energy inside our body actually extends past our skin and is the vibrational developing physiology and frequency of our body. It's more commonly referred to as our Aura, your bioplasmic body, aka Aura, has the ability to evolve rapidly and is stimulated by consciousness. The scientific understanding is that we are a combination of matter and antimatter, whereby our nervous system is electric, and that our carbon-based bodies act as this giant capacitor. Pranic practitioners and breatharians are able to use our natural electric fields and connect with our *'Auric Electromagnetic Field'* (EMF). To the average everyday person we typically refer to our EMF as our *'Chakras'*. Our Chakras energy flows in and out of our *Bioplasmic bodies* creating the human electromagnetic field, in short our bioplasmic bodies contain properties of our electromagnetic current and chakras that then either receives and feeds this energy into the meridians within our bodies or is transmitted into our environment.

The purpose of exposing you to this level of information isn't to convert you to breatharianism or to encourage you to not eat or drink, but quite simply to highlight that the most basic fundamentals to our existence should no longer be taken for granted. In their simplicity, they expose the most complex and innately flawless universal structure; that everything feeds into each other, proving that everything originates from the same source.

Every time I sit down and take that in, I can't help but show signs of humility and appreciation for the majesty of our creator and the gifts we were created with. These Six Pillars at face value were merely things we did everyday rendering their significance something that was overlooked, yet the more they were examined the new finding created powerful scientific and spiritual breakthroughs, and when they were are traced back to their origin they expose the complexity and immaculate synergy between the make-up of who we are and the entire universe.

So my final request here is for you to try and breathe intentionally and visualise your body being nourished by the oxygen in each of the breaths you breathe, your blood being alkalized and your cells singing with the *pranic energy* that is available to us every time we take a breath; and watch the difference in how your body begins to respond to every breath you breathe. One last point is that as soon as you accept the information you've just read then your *Reticular Activating System* will highlight this newfound information as important and will scan your day looking for anything that will reaffirm this newfound belief; and as a consequence you'll automatically focus on breathing better.

||||||||||||||||||||||||||||||||||||||||||||||||||||||

Breathing doesn't just keep you alive,
it feeds this incredible life force
into your physical body.

||||||||||||||||||||||||||||||||||||||||||||||||||||||

breathing for weight loss

'When you lose weight where does the weight go?'

If I were to ask you, where does the fat go when you lose weight, chances are that you'd have to pause and think about it. Your first response would probably be that you'd burn it off. How about if I told you that you actually exhale the majority of it.

Our bodies are made up of Hydrogen, Carbon and Oxygen, and I mean everything. The chemical formula for fat happens to be $C_{55} H_{104} O_6$, which effectively means 55 carbon atoms, 104 hydrogen atoms and 6 oxygen atoms.

Research done by Meerman and Brown suggests what yogis and ancient civilisations have suspected for ages. Biochemically speaking, whenever we overeat the excess energy is converted and stored in our fat cells known as adipocytes. If you wish to metabolise your stored fat cells, then specific processes in the body need to take place where the relevant hormones convert your larger fat molecules into smaller fatty acid molecules known as triglycerides. These triglycerides are then sent through the bloodstream to all the cells that can actually metabolise these fatty acids, which are now oxidised and broken down in the matrix of mitochondria which are considered to be the power generator of your cells that convert oxygen and other nutrients into energy. That's where all the enzymes required for this oxidation process of the fatty acids are located. This is an oversimplified explanation; however, the process is referred to as 'Beta Oxidation'. For this process to occur you must be able to create the need for this cycle to occur via your diet, level of activity and lifestyle.

The question still remains, where does the fat actually end up? The clinical test outlining the answer to this question ultimately found that fat plus oxygen ended up giving you Carbon Dioxide and Water formula looked like this:

$C_{55} H_{104} O_6 + 78 O_2 > 55 CO_2 + 52 H_2O$.

When people want to lose weight the biggest misconception is that we burn it up as heat. However, when we want to lose weight we lose weight in kgs which already highlights a flaw in our perception and that is energy or heat are measured by different units. Energy is measured in Kilojoules or Calories, which are extremely important as they are needed when we move, think or need to stay warm. That's not where the fat goes, but what we need to understand is that when we lose weight we are actually losing atoms. Thermodynamics says that we can't just turn atoms into nothing, the law of conservation of mass states that mass in an isolated system is neither created nor destroyed by chemical reactions or physically transformed. What that really means is that before an action and after a reaction we must have the same amount of atoms and so you can't convert fat, which is measured in kilograms, into kilojoules.

Every time you metabolise sugar you convert it into carbon dioxide and water.

Oxygen atoms can be exchanged between carbon dioxide molecules and water molecules and so what the ultimate finding was in the Meerman and Brown experiment is that 84% of the molecules will go out as carbon dioxide and 16% percent will go out as water and either through urination, respiration, perspiration or faeces. That's right, a whopping 84 percent of fat is exhaled as carbon dioxide. To put things in perspective say you lose 10 kgs or fat then 8.4 kgs of that is converted into invisible gas that you exhale. So the next time you're working out and your need for breathing increases, then make the most of that opportunity and focus on your breathing just as much as the workout.

You won't lose weight by breathing alone, however, the intention was to highlight how important breathing is to help maximise your fat loss potential.

breathing improves cardiovascular health

The importance of breathing to stay alive is obvious, but are you aware of the impacts our breath has on our cardiovascular system and its significance in being able to heal the heart in no time? Many people think of breathing as being irrelevant to the solution to heart problems, but even doctors, who prescribe medical intervention and surgery, will encourage their patients to get exercise suitable for their condition. I find it astonishing that something that comes naturally to us is overlooked as a method of healing the heart. The autonomic nervous system unconsciously regulates bodily functions, such as heart rate, digestion, respiratory rate, pupillary response, urination, and sexual arousal. Each beat of your heart is a direct result of the interplay between the two branches of the autonomic nervous system: the *sympathetic nervous system* also known as the fight or flight response, and the *parasympathetic nervous system* known as our 'rest and digest' nervous system.

The way they are actually impacted is through something referred to as the *heart rate variability*, which is the space or time between each heartbeat. You might see this as a power struggle between two of the branches of the autonomic nervous system as the sympathetic is always active and wants to increase your heart rate and pulse in an attempt to keep you alert, alive and safe. Conversely the parasympathetic is the complete opposite that wants to calm you down and slow your heart rate and pulse all in attempt to conserve energy and invest it in its primary functions of optimising your immune system, detox and improving your digestion.

Much like all the other eye-opening topics in this chapter, the reason for introducing this topic is to help you understand the significance of breathing genuinely surpasses the idea that we breath to merely stay alive. Again, once you're able to improve your breathing like everything else the impacts are profound on your mental, physical and emotional health, which includes improving your heart rate and its efficiency.

Unfortunately for most, our lives are being dictated by our perceptions, experiences and circumstances, as a result we tend to lean on being in the *fight or flight mode* most of the day which is the leading cause of a number of chronic mental and physical health problems that can just as easily be remedied by calming the body down. For example, acid reflux, chronic back pain, anxiety and depression are a few things that can be tackled with body-calming techniques.

When we're in a sympathetic fight or flight mode, the body is in a state of panic and in no way is thinking of recovery or relaxation, but rather, how to survive and stay alive. If that sounds like you then the best way you can combat that is to retrain yourself to breathe again to where the diaphragm moves in and out freely and pushes the viscera (internal organs) kind of like the plant or vegetation on the bottom of the ocean that moves with the current. Conversely when we breathe under stress, we tend to take shallow breaths and overcompensate by engaging our shoulders and chest, which reduces the oxygen we could get with every breath we breathe.

The most effective way to improve breathing and the oxygen uptake into our bodies is to focus on diaphragmatic breathing. The diaphragm is the most efficient breathing muscle that's located at the base of the lungs. As you inhale, the diaphragm contracts, which then produces a negative back pressure in the thorax. And as a result it creates a vacuum like effect, drawing air into your lungs. Another important factor to consider is how important breathing is for our organs in our bellies.

Read on a little further and we'll address exactly how to retrain yourself to breathe properly.

breathing and anxiety

Is your breathing causing you anxiety? One of anxiety's common triggers is an overstimulated sympathetic nervous system. Most people breathe shallow, meaning that you are typically breathing from your mouth and that the chest predominately moves and not the diaphragm. When we have had overexaggerated anxious experiences we begin to unconsciously hold our breath or breathe with shallow breaths. This breathing pattern can over-excite the sympathetic nervous system and trigger an anxious state of being. The point here is that we have developed a habit of dysfunctional breathing, which may be causing the same biological experiences as though you were experiencing some level of anxiety. Think about it, if your everyday breathing is likened to the same breathing pattern as though you're having an anxiety attack then the body will immediately produce all the relevant physiological and biochemical responses to suit your state of being.

During an emergency we inevitably trigger a state of hyperventilation because our breathing rate and pattern changes, as we begin to breathe shorter, shallower and more rapidly, the typical symptoms experienced during a panic attack are:

> dizziness
> shortness of breath
> a lump in the throat
> tingling or numbness in the hands or feet
> nausea
> confusion

The good news is that when you improve your breathing rate and breathing pattern, you immediately begin to reverse the symptoms, by activating and stimulating the body's parasympathetic response and immediately intensifying the relaxation response. It's also known as the rest and digest response. A little hack to help you activate the parasympathetic nervous system is to inhale from the nose. That's because there is a high density of parasympathetic nerve endings in the nose and as the air you inhale tickles your nasal hairs and passes the turbinates (a part of your nasal passageway) it activates the calming response centre in the brain and you immediately begin to calm down. As soon as that happens you will immediately start reversing the processes that may have led you to feel any of the above-mentioned symptoms.

so how do i breathe better?

'Stress Causes Disruption To Our Breathing Patterns'

Here's a quick recap in highlighting how significant breathing is. Without oxygen or air for three minutes your brain will be in a lot of trouble. You can survive without food or water for a lot longer than 3 minutes but not without air.

The intention behind the topics selected in this *Pillar* has been to increase your awareness from this once perceived belief that we merely breathe to stay alive, to having a brand new outlook and appreciation that when we're able to improve how we breathe, that not only will we increase the oxygen uptake into every cell and how they function, but that every single function of the body improves immediately as all of our physiological systems are dependent upon breathing for life and that breathing properly can also positively influence our psychology. Lastly, for the spiritual beings out there, breathing has a profound impact on how energy flows through our meridian system.

So how do I breathe properly?

To start retraining yourself to breathe your way back to good health, place one hand on your stomach and the other hand on your chest. Now start practicing expanding your belly which means to basically let your diaphragm drop. Your diaphragm sits under your rib cage, we mentioned earlier that as you inhale the diaphragm contracts which produces a negative pressure in the thorax that causes a vacuum drawing air into your body.

As we inhale, the diaphragm contracts and needs to have the ability to drop. For this to happen your stomach will have to be able to expand outward. While pulling your stomach in has been used as a method for 'good posture', it's important that you let your diaphragm rise and fall naturally with your breathing.

breathing from your belly!

To complete a belly breath, place one hand on your belly and the other hand on your chest. For the first two thirds of your breath, the hand on your belly should be moving. Only on the last third of your breath should the hand on the chest start to move. On the exhale, just simply relax and make sure you let that breath out fully as most people don't fully exhale. I am not asking you to force it out, however whilst you practice your new breathing pattern quite simply on your exhale allow your abdominals to relax and empty that air out, so that you're able to move all the stale air out of your body, then inhale and simply repeat the process.

Make it a regular practice, as it will take time to retrain your breathing pattern to where you no longer focus on the breathing exercise. Remember it takes approximately 30 days to redevelop new movement or breathing patterns.

Great news is that if you become reactive to your environment and start to become anxious, implement or shift your focus to these new breathing patterns; it has been found to calm you down quite quickly.

4-7-8 Breathing and the Vagus Nerve

> 'As you continue to breathe and notice the air moving in and out of your lungs you may think about the role that oxygen plays in nourishing your body and bathing your tissues with the energy you need to feel alive and engaged.'
> ~ Dr Bessel Van Der Kolk

The vagus nerve is a nerve that is a modulator of the brain as it connects the brainstem to the body. The role of the *vagus nerve* in the parasympathetic nervous system is to slow the sympathetic stress response. There has been plenty of evidence indicating that if it's activated properly that it can immediately reduce anxiety, or at least help manage anxiety and mild depression. Breathing is an incredibly efficient way to help activate the vagus nerve properly.

The 4-7-8 breathing technique is one of the best techniques I've found as it not only helps activate the vagus nerve but I've also found that it can help with reducing and improving how you manage your anxiety. When done correctly it will put you in an altered state of consciousness. It can also help you get to sleep when your mind starts randomly racing out of control the moment you put your head on the pillow. Believe it or not this exact same breathing technique can also help curb hunger cravings when you feel like you're out of control and binge eating. Lastly if you've become highly reactive and at times tend to become aggressive then this breathing technique will also help you manage it. It's for these reasons I thought I would suggest you try this for yourself.

How do I do it? Before starting the breathing pattern, adopt a comfortable sitting position ideally with your back nice and straight, place the tip of the tongue on the tissue right behind the top front teeth, and keep it there through the entire exercise. Lastly Exhale through your mouth around your tongue; try pursing your lips slightly otherwise you may run out of breath before the count of 8.

To use the 4-7-8 techniques, the following steps should all be carried out in the cycle of one breath:

1. First step is to completely exhale any air that's in your lungs through your mouth until you feel like you're ready to take a new breath.
2. Next step is to inhale silently through your nose as you count to four in your head.
3. Then, hold your breath for 7 seconds.
4. Next, exhale from your mouth through pursed lips for the count of 8 seconds.

That is now considered 1 repetition, repeat that 10 more times to complete 1 set.

The reason why this is so effective is that when you inhale from the nose, you immediately stimulate the parasympathetic nervous system to put you in a calm state of mind, when you hold your breath for 7 seconds you immediately activate the lymphatic system and when you exhale for twice as long as you've inhaled you not only let out all the air and stale air in your lungs but you also help eliminate the toxins.

It's recommended to use this technique at least twice a day to help maximise the benefits you get from the 4-7-8 breathing. I would suggest completing one set when you first wake up and then again more sets before you go to bed.

Initially you may start feeling a little lightheaded after doing this for the first few times, I assure you it'll pass and it's only because your body is processing toxins whilst oxygenating your cells. I would advise you to be either sitting or lying down to prevent you from falling over if you're susceptible to getting dizzy.

The longer and more frequently you use the technique, the more effective it will become.

chapter 10:
the fourth pillar – hydration

Water is something most either love to swim in or surf in. Water has a calming effect when we're under pressure or not feeling well because of its sensory deprivation abilities. I love to drink it.

Conventional science tells us that water is fundamental to our existence with two thirds of the earth's surface being covered by water and the human body consisting of 75 percent of it the truth of the matter is that water affects and impacts 99% of life. Based on my last remark it's evidently clear that water is one of the prime molecules responsible for life on earth. Water circulates through the land just as it does through the human body, transporting, dissolving, replenishing nutrients and organic matter, while carrying away waste material. Further in the body, it regulates the activities of fluids, tissues, cells, lymph, blood and glandular secretions.

An average adult body contains 42 litres of water and if you experience a small loss of 2.7 litres you can suffer from dehydration, display symptoms of irritability, fatigue, nervousness, dizziness, weakness, headaches and potentially cause colitis, kidney stones, bladder and urinary tract infections. We're taught in school that water is a basic molecule made up of Hydrogen and Oxygen. Let me show how water is much more complex in its structure and profound in the way it impacts us and the world as we know it.

So far it's all pretty straight forward and maybe a little boring. Here's where I start to lay it all out and showcase how water is far from a basic molecule. I personally have been blown away after my extensive research on how water impacts our lives and the universe and is why I delicately chose the topics outlined in this chapter, so that it too can have the same impact on you, rather than just give you all the boring biological facts of how water plays an important role in our health and wellbeing. Too many have already been there and done that.

My intention is to make you appreciate the realisation that the best things in life for us are completely free and water is now my favourite natural resource that I use in my arsenal to a happier and healthier me. Since the beginning of our creation water has been cycling through everything that inhabits this earth, from rocks, plants, bacteria, the oceans, storm clouds, animals and so much more. However, here is why I love water, it doesn't not follow or fit into the conventional wisdom of science. For starters we know that water is comprised of hydrogen and oxygen atoms and is a liquid on earth, yet the laws of chemistry state that water should be a gas and not a liquid based on the temperatures we have here on earth. Equally to 'Physicists' water is also abnormal, due to the fact that as other materials or molecules cool down in temperature they begin to contract, however that's not the case with water; it expands as it freezes. Water's density actually gets lighter as the volume increases which allows ice to float on water for example in the Antarctic.

Think about this for a second, the frozen ice that is at -4 degrees Celsius now floats on the surface of the water that is usually around zero degrees Celsius. The interesting fact is that scientists have also found that water at zero degrees Celsius can also float on water that is slightly warmer than it, for example, at 4 degrees Celsius. That intelligence gives all the marine life an opportunity to thrive and a great example of this was during the earth's various ice ages, when marine life was flourishing.

If water was as basic as we believe it to have been, then you would think that at the first sign of winter based on *'conventional science'* is that as soon as the top layers of the lake would start to freeze, it would continue to freeze until every part of that lake was frozen, which would cause all the marine life and marine plants to simply perish. But this isn't what happens. Another amazing fact is that water molecules can float upwards against the force of gravity, for example when you add ice to your glass of water or choice of beverage, it always somehow ends up at the surface. The reason I make this distinction is that if water didn't have this level of intelligence where its molecules are able to stick together and pull themselves up against the force of gravity in your body, then how would oxygen and nutrients ever reach your brain? That is the exact same process that allows plants to also get the water to travel from the deepest part of their roots into areas like the leaves and branches so that they are nourished and can grow in the amazing sunlight.

One more interesting fact is that water is the second most common molecule in our solar system and dare I say, where there is water there is energy; and even more interestingly where there is water there may even be life.

So you see the colourless, odourless, featureless and boring glass of water you overlook is so much more profound than you've ever imagined. I've only just started to scrape the surface of learning and appreciating the most amazing molecule I've been privileged to research.

the triple point of water

As we've established, science in schools teaches us that there are three phases to water which are solid, liquid, and gas. We also know that as water cools it begins to freeze into a solid. Conversely if we heat it up it'll evaporate into steam or vapor.

Now, did you know that the speed and temperature in which water either freezes or evaporates or remains in its liquid state is not absolute, it's actually largely affected by the air pressure. For example, the boiling point of water that is reported in all science textbooks is at 1 atmospheric pressure and that's basically sea level. At sea level water is known to boil at 100 degrees Celsius and so if you reduce the atmospheric pressure water will now boil at 98 degrees Celsius and if you continue to reduce the atmospheric pressure again it'll boil a lot quicker.

Now why does this matter? It matters because there is an atmospheric pressure and a temperature for which water, ice and steam all co exist and it's called the triple point of water. Can you imagine that, looking at a glass of water and at one very precise temperature and air pressure that glass of water will steam up, have ice circling in it whilst still remaining a liquid? Tell me that doesn't blow your mind?

Unfortunately there really isn't much research or content on this topic and the reason I made reference to this point in the chapter is to prepare you for the fact that we go through this world oblivious to just how amazing the world around us is. Despite this we live life at what we call room temperature and one atmospheric pressure and yet we allow these limiting factors to define our life and our experiences and how we interact with that environment.

The reality of our lives is far from what we've been misled to believe and that once you expand your way of thinking you will not only appreciate the blessings and gifts you have; you'll be able to genuinely cultivate your soul and become more yourself, change and transform just like the water that shows you that when you allow yourself to be surrounded by the right atmosphere, the right temperature that you're not bound to only one experience in life.

And that just as all three forms of the water co-exist at all times, then so does your mind, body and spirit, but it's the environment that determines how well you're able to welcome new opportunities and new possibilities.

water for weight loss

As we've now established the majority of us is made of water! That means if you regulate your water intake and really work on prioritising it during your day, you can contribute to improving weight loss whilst also investing in your overall health.

By drinking more water, you will:

Increase Resting Caloric Expenditure: A study of overweight women, who increased their water intake over a 12-month period, lost 2-3 kgs for the year without making any other changes to their lives. In all the study participants resting energy expenditure had shown to increase by up to 30% within ten minutes of drinking water. So by simply drinking water, your natural metabolic energy burning process kickstarts regardless of your physical movement.

Eat Less: Sometimes those moments when you assume that you are hungry or when you get those hunger pains in your stomach is actually your body crying out for water and not food.

Here's a tip to try, simply drink a glass or two of room temperature water 10-20 min before any meal and what you will find is that it may help prevent you from overeating.

Have Muscle Fuel: Your muscles are 80% water. If you want to provide them with energy for exercise and movement, you *'need'* to start with what they are predominantly made of and that's water. Remember that the more lean muscle you progressively add to your body, the higher your resting metabolic process will become and water is a great way to develop leaner and healthier muscle tissue.

As you can see, every bodily process, from digestion to the functioning of the brain, involves water. And remember that your joints, your vital organs, your blood flow, and your respiratory systems flow and function smoothly when you are optimally hydrated.

Dr Masaru Emoto

Dr Masaru Emoto is one of the most important water researchers the world has known, the Japanese scientist revolutionised the idea that our thoughts and intentions impact our external environment. Dr Emoto's research provided scientific evidence of how the molecular structure in water transforms when it is exposed to sound, thoughts, words and intentions.

The doctor became extremely interested in the molecular structure of water and what effects it, he set up a series of studies and applied mental stimuli and then photographed the water samples with a dark field microscope. He would collect water from dams around Japan and then photograph the water. He would take another photograph of the same water after it received blessings from Zen Buddhist monks, and he then began to print out words and tape the words to bottles of distilled water, for example the word 'love' or 'thank you', and let them sit overnight, and then examined the differences in how these experiments affected the crystalline structure of the water.

His research demonstrated how water exposed to loving and compassionate words and intention resulted in aesthetically pleasing physical molecular formations in the water, whilst when the water was exposed to negative, fearful and toxic words and intentions resulted in disconnected, disfigured, and 'unpleasant' physical molecular formations. His studies also demonstrated how certain types of sound, like classical music, generate beautiful crystalline patterns, while heavy metal music, generate ugly and distorted crystalline formations.

Dr Emoto says that the thought or the intent is the driving force behind this and that when he would freeze the water to get the photograph of the crystalline structures, as soon as the temperature of water would go back to zero degrees Celsius, the crystalline shape would then disappear. He then said that this image must be the design of the vibration. This scientific research could show that what we think, what we feel and what we believe affects everything around us, including water. If we are made up predominately of water, then how do you think that these negative words and intentions will impact us? Doesn't it make you wonder if thoughts can do that to water then imagine what those same thoughts are doing to us?

After reading about what consciousness is in *Chapter 12* then I would ask you to revisit this topic and that along your journey that you process all this newfound information at your own pace, because the realisation at the end of this is that you are truly an amazing creation and capable of so much more than you had ever given yourself credit for. I pray that you find yourself and eventually help others around you to do the same.

Lastly, Dr Emoto stated in an interview that this universe including our bodies are made from water, and that he believes if a human being's consciousness is beautiful then his or her universe must also become beautiful. If the human being's consciousness is not beautiful then their universe must resemble their beliefs. Ultimately he is stating that he believes that water is this life force and is the messenger of God.

> 'Water records information,
> and while circulating throughout
> the earth distributes information.
> This water sent from the universe
> is full of information about life...
> Understanding the fact that
> we are essentially water
> is the key to uncovering
> the mysteries of the universe.'
> ~ Masaru Emoto

water memory

If I have not challenged your perceptual personal truths enough already, here's another one to process. Although we have highlighted that water plays an important part in our existence, the truth is that water plays a much greater role in life. One that is far greater than we could have ever imagined or even comprehended. Water has the ability to reproduce the properties of any substance it has been exposed to and that's because water has *memory* and that statement completely defies conventional science and the understanding of physical chemistry.

I believe that learning about the mechanisms of life is extremely important and is why I continue to deliver this type of content. And I get *'water having memory'* is a theory that may be a little hard to digest, however, in researching and writing this book over the space of the last 7 years, what I have come to work out is that we have three truths. The first is our *'personal truth'* which is guided by the aroma of our personal experiences and perception. The second truth is a *'political truth'* which is influenced by the public opinion and what the hierarchy wants us to believe and the then there is my favourite, *'The objective truth'*. The thing I love most about the objective truth is that it remains the truth no matter what.

We are all susceptible to a bias and I encourage you to be a sceptic, simply because a true sceptic will be sceptical about anything they're unsure of. However, when they recognise that the information makes sense and is logical then it'll become valid enough to change their mind and that's all I've intended to do throughout this journey you've taken with me.

This book is about equipping you with the tools needed to better understand the new you and more importantly be able to communicate with others and use your story to inspire them to also understand themselves. And in turn hope that they use their story to inspire someone else. This is how we all co-create greatness.

Conventional science and classical physics believes that water does not carry any signal, however there was a test done by professors where the end results showed that water can receive and transmit signals. That is the objective truth. For example, world renowned researcher Luc Montagnier loaded the data and signals of water molecules that had been charged with the DNA of a patient into a solution. The solution was diluted to such a high degree that not even a single molecule of the DNA information was present in the water. The only influencing factor left in this test was the structure of the water molecules that was emitting its own distinct signals. This was only possible because the diluted water of the DNA had retained the memory of the DNA traces in the form of electromagnetic signals according to professor Montagnier. Here's where it gets really interesting is that Professor Montagnier now transfers the digital file of this DNA signal in the water to his computer and then sends it through the internet to another country, so that they can reproduce the exact same structure of emitting signals in a totally different sample of water.

The file was sent to a university in Italy that specialises in molecular biology. The lab in Italy took the signal that was recorded in France, that signal was then processed from the computer and sent through to a tube of purified water, the experiment according to the professor is that the water in the test tube will listen to the signals and memorise them.

In Italy the tube of purified water was prepared for the experiment by being placed inside a solenoid and then placed in a cylinder to eliminate the possibility of any interference of radiation that could be in the lab. Then the signal from the internet was played into to the test tube of water in Italy for approx 1 hour.

The water was now placed in a PCR (polymerase chain reaction) machine, a method that's used in molecular biology that ultimately copies DNA sequences.

The result was a breathtaking success. The DNA was able to be reconstituted from water that had simply picked up the frequency of the signal-emitting DNA-infused water that was sent from another country and through the internet. This revolutionary experiment was so profound that it created a new vision of how water plays a much greater role in our bodies than it was once perceived. Science experiments have now established that water could have the capacity to store and transfer information.

the spirit of water

Now that your past perceptions have been challenged with some impressive content, backed by scientific facts, it may just be time to explore something else. I genuinely believe that water is so much more profound than we give it credit for and I'm hoping that the next time someone says 'Oh, it's just some water,' you'll know how to respond to that.

Looking at water objectively, what do we really know about it? The obvious answers are that we know it's the most prevalent and common substance on earth and that every living species and organism comes from water. We also know that the human body is up to 95 percent water and that quite simply without water life would not exist. For example, in science there is a theory that describes a *'primordial soup'* in which it has been claimed that all organic molecules originated in water before evolving out of the oceans, millions of years later, into the world around us as we know it.

Water doesn't just flow in oceans, lakes and rivers; our entire atmosphere is made up of water. Some questions that showcase water as an intelligence that still continues to blow scientists away are, why does water have the highest surface tension of all liquids that allows objects including humans to float on it? Why can water rise against the force of gravity through the trunks of trees against an immense amount of atmospheric pressure? Why is water the only element that expands when it freezes and shrinks when it heats up? It's these kinds of questions that have been left unanswered, that have the world of science still puzzled, as science has given us no conclusive answer.

The benefit of this is that it's allowing us to become open to exploring water in ways that may challenge the status quo, which has led to some extremely impressive and miraculous discoveries. One of the biggest revelations and what's making water so impressive is the way in which water structures its molecules. That discovery allowed us to see water in a different light, rather than the once perceived theory that waters' chemical composition was the only important thing we needed to know. This only allowed us to see water as something we drink and shower in. Water is so impressive that it's able to join its molecules into groups or clusters. Scientists have discovered that these clusters formed the water's 'memory', which allows the water to record and even more impressively recall the relationship it experienced in any of its environments.

That's right! This simple cup of water changes its structure when you turn on the light, it again changes its structure when you change the environment and although the glass of water appears to just be water, its structured much like your nervous system that responds and reacts to any environmental irritation. One of the profound scientific findings regarding the cluster is that in general, a cluster left as a specific group or arrangement of molecules can only survive a certain amount of time in that form. With water, scientists have found that the structure of the molecules water created had molecules leaving and other molecules joining, which allows the clusters the ability to last a very long time.

The stability of the cluster structure that water was able to create and how it was able to create it, had now confirmed the hypothesis that water is capable of storing and recording information. Professor Roy Rustum likened the structure of water to the alphabet, and that the alphabet alone, much like the molecular structure of water, is only an alphabet. However, it's the way that letters are arranged in the water that makes up the sentences and words that we then can understand, and that's exactly the same with water and the way it structures its molecules. The amazing thing is that this information can change every time the environment the water is exposed to changes.

Take into consideration what you know about water and its intelligence. After all the scientific experiments carried out by Dr Masaru Emoto and scientists alike, try to imagine what is happening to the water that enters our home and how it's affected by its journey.

If, much like us, the water adopts of all the stresses, fears and angers in its and our environment, by the time its sent through the corroded pipes and then massacred with an infusion of toxic chemicals, for example chlorine and fluoride, what kind of impact on the water and its memory do you think it'll have? How beneficial would the water be loaded with all the wrong information for your cells, every time the cell splits and goes through the process of mitosis? Those are the same cells that have made up every part of you and me.

All I am saying is that water is life, and evidently has healing benefits that up until today still haven't been fully understood or recognised by science, throughout the book the evidence has been delicately worded and delivered to you into digestible bite-sized pieces that clearly highlight that all healing intentions become a reality with well chosen words, thoughts and most importantly, beliefs.

Water, like everything else, carries its own frequency that vibrates at a certain rate. Since our bodies are made up of these 'water filled' cells that vibrate at different frequencies, it wouldn't be that unusual for there to be some frequencies that have come from thoughts, feelings, emotions, even the 'foods' and 'water' we consume, that are out of coherence with the cells in our bodies, and that negatively influenced the way our cells behave and respond, mentally, physically and emotionally. I guess what I'm really alluding to is that water is so much more than we can understand. I believe that water is genuinely the messenger of God and that there's so much more to water than meets the eye, which is what science is only just starting to discover and that Water is as *Spiritual* as it is *Physical*.

Water is energy and all energy can be transmuted, In *Physics* there's a law known as 'the Law of Perpetual Transmutation of Energy'. This basically states that energy is universal and that energy is all around and within us, and more importantly that it is transmutable, which means that energy can transfer into another matter and then back again into its pure state of energy.

This means that energy, therefore everything (including us) cannot die, it can only change forms. What this law tells us is that we all have the power to change our life experiences, situations and conditions. We all have that creative power and can use these universal laws in our favour. The immediate and simple answer to prevent destructive vibrations in our water is to bless it which will change the vibration pattern immediately much like priests, mystics, and shamans, whereby they blessed the water with a prayer of thanks and gratitude.

Thoughts are energy. By focussing your thoughts consciously in a certain direction, that energy transforms into the form your thoughts are creating. Physical forms can manifest from the energy of your thoughts. After all that has been discussed with Dr Emoto's and professor Montagnier's research (how water stores memory; how water has the ability to change its structure of molecular clusters to suit the environment and its experiences), why not start to focus on positive energy transmutation into that water before you drink it? It will have a completely new and positive effect on your cells, which are effectively the makeup of you.

Quality drinking water that you appreciate will have such a profound impact on your health and wellbeing. I personally have adopted Dr Emoto's philosophy, I write words like Love, Joy, Prosperity and Gratitude on my bottle and when I drink it, I genuinely feel I'm bringing healthier energy into my personal being. I feel as though I can think clearer and I feel healthier. I'm able to add a higher frequency of energy to myself. When you lift yourself you immediately lift everyone else around you.

chapter 11:
the fifth pillar – sleep

How do I fall asleep faster, how do I sleep deeper? Why is it we're talking about sleep in a self-help book? And when you get a bad night's sleep, how do you feel the next day? Sleep plays a critical role in how your brain and body performs and that lack of sleep hurts all the cognitive processes as it impairs attention, alertness, concentration, and reasoning.

Notice when you are updating your smartphone, the smart phone won't allow you to use it while it's uploading all its new data into the hard drive. That is the exact same process with us and sleep, scientific research reveals that sleep is essential after learning any newfound data that goes into our nervous system. The most important part of learning anything is getting the optimal sleep so that your brain and body is ready to soak up all the new information you collect for the day.

The information I'm referring to isn't just information we learn out of a book but rather the information or the stimuli that comes at us from our surrounding environment as the body and the mind are always adapting. That's how we have kept ourselves alive since the beginning of our creation.

Without the right amounts of sleep your brain and body become sluggish and very unproductive. To put things in perspective, I was once challenged to write five chapters in one night. In typical fashion I used that challenge as a means to push myself past my own limits and not only finish the five chapters but complete the whole book I was writing. I stayed up all night and throughout the process, I found that my rate of efficiency dropped whilst the rate of mistakes increased. I would combat this by having cold showers to wake me up and stimulate my own natural version of a Red Bull energy drink to keep me going. I ended up finishing it at 7 am then going straight back to the class the next morning to work on test subjects and learn new information. What I found is that I was unable to focus and take in any new information for the rest of the day until I slept from 5 pm that night until 7 am the following morning, before I went back into class where I now was able to soak in every bit of new information and add my own personal take on the topic and give it a newfound flavour that would become the base of creating this life changing program.

The reason was simple, as I now started researching what goes on in the brain that produces these types of learning disabilities the ultimate finding was that on both sides of your brain there is a structure that sits there known as the hippocampus, which is like the informational receiver box of the brain. It is exceptional at receiving new memory files and holding onto them. When you are sleep deprived the body-mind will shut down your ability to receive any new information until it figures out what caused you to not sleep and shifts you into a sympathetic fight or flight mode. This renders you unable to effectively commit any new experience or knowledge to your memory.

So you see, the disruption of 'Deep Sleep' is a significantly underappreciated factor that heavily contributes to any type of cognitive decline. The great news is that you're about to learn how to capitalise on being able to continually get your brain to operate at peak performance. What actually restores and enhances your ability to consume and retain new information every day quite simply comes down to these big brain wave development patterns that happen when we have deep sleep. During deep sleep, there are bursts of electrical activity known as sleep spindles and it's the coherence of these two mechanisms that help improve our ability to retain data when we sleep. This is where the brain now takes the short-term memories and stores them as long-term memories/synaptic connections.

Lastly sleep is by no means an optional luxury where we get to choose whether or not we should get some sleep, Sleep is a biological necessity. It may just be worth appreciating and prioritising regular sleep times.

stages of sleep

There are four stages or cycles of sleep that are recognised in two main categories, the first is Rapid Eye Movement (REM) and the second is Non-Rapid Eye Movement, Non-REM sleep.

Your sleep cycle is a progression through these various stages of both NREM sleep and REM sleep. Typically, a person would begin a sleep cycle every 90-120 minutes and it averages between four and five cycles in the time, or hours, they've spent asleep.

If I were to use an analogy, it'd be that your sleep cycles are likened to a manual or stick shift car, and your sleep is the freeway we intend on traveling on. Now we can just go from turning on the car into 4th gear. The car would not run efficiently and start to shake and splatter or maybe even stall the engine. The natural thing to do is to progress through the gears until we get to the optimal ratio and then we can cruise on the freeway.

That's the exact same thing with our sleep cycles. One does not go straight from deep sleep to REM sleep. Rather, a sleep cycle progresses through the stages of non-REM sleep from light to deep sleep, then reverses back from deep sleep to light sleep, ending with time in REM sleep before starting over in light sleep again.

The optimal time to go to sleep is usually between 10:30pm to no later than 11pm to get into the first wave or cycle. If you miss that first wave you may have to wait until you catch it again and at times you could be super tired at night, then all of a sudden you're extremely awake because you had to finish off a movie and went past your bedtime. Usually you say, 'Oh, I'm now restless because I'm overly tired.' That could be because you missed your first stage of the sleep cycle.

There are these little on and off switches or triggers that cause you to go to sleep or wake up that work with your suprachiasmatic nucleus that's responsible for controlling your circadian rhythms. This is just a fancy way of saying your body clock that is regulated by light and darkness.

Sleepers cyclically will pass through all four stages: 1, 2, 3, and then REM (rapid eye movement) sleep. A complete sleep cycle takes an average of 90 to 110 minutes, with each stage lasting between 5 to 15 minutes. The first sleep cycles of each night have relatively short REM sleeps and long periods of deep sleep but later in the night, REM periods lengthen and deep sleep time decreases.

Stage 1 is the lightest stage of Non-Rapid Eye Movement sleep as it's defined by the presence of slow eye movements. It's typically the drowsy sleep. In the second stage slow moving eye rolls discontinue as your 'Brain Waves' continue to slow with specific bursts of rapid activity known as 'sleep spindles', intermixed with sleep structures known as 'K complexes'. Both sleep spindles and K complexes serve as protection for the brain from awakening from sleep. Body temperature begins to decrease and the heart rate begins to slow.

The real rejuvenating and the most restorative stage of sleep is stage 3, and it consists of delta waves.

REM sleep, also known as rapid eye movement, is most commonly known as the dreaming stage. Eye movements are rapid, moving from side to side and brain waves are more active than in Stages 2 and 3 of sleep. Awakenings and arousals can occur more easily in REM; being woken during a REM period can leave one feeling groggy or overly sleepy.

Research is still a relatively young field; scientists didn't discover REM sleep until 1953. Before this time science believed that most of the brain activity ceased during sleep, which shows how far science has advanced as the new teaching proves that deprivation of REM sleep is one of the leading contributors to mental illnesses like clinical depression, and that it can also lead to insanity.

Brain Wave frequencies during these sleep cycles at stage 1 of Non-REM sleep, is between 4-8 HZ and is when we get into theta brain waves. This stage of sleep is usually only 5% of your total sleep time as an adult. Stage 2 of the Non-REM cycle is likened to stage one, except we now have the rapid burst activity of K complexes, which create brief large spikes of activity and the spindle waves, which are rapid rhythmic bursts of activity when the spindle waves are buzzing creating their magic. During this time the frequency increases a little and usually sits between 4-15 HZ. This cycle usually counts for about 45% of your total sleep time. Before the spindle waves start to slow down at stage 3, where the brain wave activity is now at delta waves, it has the lowest frequency at 1-4HZ, but has the highest amplitude. This is the deepest stage of sleep where you will lose all your bodily awareness and it will count for 25% of your total sleep time before you move into the fun stage of sleep. During REM, which also accounts for 25% of your total sleep and is where vivid dreaming occurs and is where we facilitate memories processing the brain wave activity in REM sleep are low voltage and high frequency that mostly resemble beta brain waves.

I genuinely wanted to add this section in to scientifically show you how everything, including sleep, has energy that vibrates at a certain frequency even when we sleep. So that the more you are aware of your energy and can improve and stabilize it through all this newfound knowledge, then typically you would be in total control of your mental, physical and your emotional health.

sleep and weight loss

'Sleep' is the missing transformational component you've been looking for.

Sleep is something that we do for about a third of our lives, and for it to take up that amount of significant time then you'd have to think that it would be pretty important. Having said that, isn't it funny that scientific studies show how obesity is at an all time high whilst our sleep quality and duration has been shown to be at an all time low? *Conclusive Scientific Research* now shows that there's a direct relationship between these two counterparts. If sleep is an integral part to losing weight and feeling good, then, why not effectively take advantage of the easiest part of losing weight?

The one important fact that has been scientifically proven about sleep is that it affects the metabolic process, there's a 1:1 relationship between sleep and metabolic activity. When you're sleep deprived the last thing you look for are carrot and celery sticks. Think about it for a second, look at the types of places open at 2am in the morning. You don't usually see people eating hummus and tofu, you see people eating pizza, kebabs or heating up the microwaved food at the local 7-Eleven.

The best way to maximise your fat burning potential is to focus on your natural sleep wave patterns that occur between 10pm and 6am. During that time period, our bodies go through neurogenic and hormonal repair cycles, which are imperative for growth and tissue repair. Hormones are chemical messengers that communicate information between all the cells in your body. Hormones bridge together your cells for the sole purpose of keeping you in a state of balance – 'Homeostasis'.

Why is this important? It's important because, for you to make the most out of being in the fat burning state, the right hormones have to communicate the right information throughout the cells in your body. If you miss sleep throughout these times, you can put yourself in a sympathetic state that craves sugars and other stimulants as well as weakens your immune system. Let's face it, your body doesn't change when you're working out or eating well, your body changes during sleep. Sleep is when growth and development happen and is the ultimate anabolic state. When you're sleeping, your body releases reparative enzymes, which are biochemical catalysts. Enzymes are the key to life and must be present for any process to occur as they make the hormone communication possible and is why when you're sleeping, your body repairs itself, resets the digestive system, and stabilizes hormones that help your metabolism to perform at its peak levels.

There was a case study on how *sleep helps transform your body* performed by the National Institute of Health (nih.gov) regarding fat loss where they took a group of individuals and placed them on a boring calorie restricted diet and then gave them 8 and a half hours of sleep per night on average. They traced and recorded the metrics.

They then took the exact same group of people and kept the same reduced caloric diet, however, they reduced the amount of sleep they had by three hours, so now they were sleep deprived at only 5 and a half hours of sleep per night on average. They again tracked and recorded all their metrics.

The conclusion of the study revealed that the when the group had 8 and a half hours of sleep per day lost 55% more body fat then when they were sleep deprived. The point I'd like you to take from this is that if losing weight is a focal point of yours, although all of the Six Pillars play a part in creating the most impressive looking and feeling you, sleep is the most impressive way to burn more body fat. There is no other process that has a stronger bearing on your hormones than sleep does.

why can't we sleep

Sleep deprivation is so common nowadays and yet is one of the things most ignored. Our mentality these days of not sleeping gives us bragging rights. For example, when you tell your friends you pulled an all-nighter, appealing to their desire for success. I totally get it, being a driven soul myself, but even a Ferrari needs rest and servicing. Scientists worldwide are now calling sleep deprivation a global emerging epidemic as statistics show that globally 40% of people experience some form of sleep deprivation. Its side effects include heart attack, stroke, depression, weight gain and even premature death.

Sleep is the foundation of where everything in life flows; from our creativity, performance, health and wellbeing. Isn't it alarming that it's the most overlooked thing when it comes to how we look, feel and perform? That is why it is super important and you understand why poor sleep patterns happen and genuinely work on your solution.

Before we go any further I'd like to randomly throw in a case study and potential self-realisation that you actually know now so much more than you thought you did.

Meet Trev. Trev is a tradie that worries all the time, literally worries about everything until he found himself in the back of an ambulance after his doctor said he was suffering a heart attack. Trev was complaining of heavy pressures on his chest, and so when he was admitted into hospital and after running extensive tests the doctor at the hospital walks in and says, 'great news, you are healthy as can be and never suffered a heart attack; just some really bad anxiety'. The doctor went on to ask him, why does a healthy man like you suffer from extreme anxiety? What is your life like?

And that's when he began to tell the doctor about his daily routine. He said, 'Doc, I'm not sure, but when I wake up the first thing I do on my way to work is to have an energy drink and a donut. I also have a couple more cans throughout the day as I find it keeps me working more efficiently.' Trev then disclosed how he has take out and fast food almost every day as it's just convenient. He craves sugar every night. Trev then finished off by saying, 'Doc, my mind is always racing and I need to stay active and busy; and Doc, for some reason I have trouble sleeping.'

'Even when I'm super exhausted I still only manage 4 hours of sleep every night.'

Now I can almost guarantee that every single one of you reading this book could help this case study almost immediately, and that you have figured out that the first thing we need to address is the fact that Trev can't get his mind to slow down. While there could be many biological causes of poor sleep, most times the biggest causes are nutritional, that effectively translate into hormonal issues and psychological processes that happen outside of our conscious awareness. As we know, our brains are hard wired to instantly identify negative information and the more worried and anxious we become throughout the day, the less likely we are to enjoy a well rested sleep.

I could go on and on about why we can't sleep and back it with scientific evidence and data, but the truth is that I bet you already know how to improve your sleep; regardless you'll be provided with suggestions later in this chapter. By genuinely implementing the Six Pillar system outlined in this book you will have all the tools to combat every ailment of a mental, physical or emotional issue. All we need to focus on is balance. Our lives are so primed with fear, toxins, stresses and so many distractions that we all have lost our way and if your mind is all over the place then how do you think the rest of your body will respond? It's kind of like having a pack of dogs and if the pack leader is calm and poised then the rest of the pack will be settled and balanced. But if the pack leader is heightened, stressed, and worried all the time the rest of the pack will be unsettled and it won't be long before the pack leader will get challenged for their position.

dreams

We've all heard dream quotes that inspire us like *'Follow your dreams'*, *'dreams can come true'*, *'dare to dream'*. So where do dreams come from?

Why is it we have dreams and what does it mean if I see rain in my dreams? One of the prevailing perspectives on dreams is the hypothesis that we dream about things that we've experienced whilst we're awake. After a great deal of scientific research we still don't have any definitive answers. However, what we do have are some interesting theories and one of them is that we dream to fulfil our wishes. In the early 1900s Sigmund Freud said in his research is that all of our dreams and nightmares are a collection of images that we've collected from our day to day lives and experiences. Accordingly, our dreams have a symbolic meaning, which he then states 'relate to fulfilling our subconscious desires'. Take that in for a second. If all of these images are a symbolic representation of our subconscious thoughts and desires, then that confirms that we become what we think about all the time.

So can you imagine what happens to your life when you add the subconscious programs, desires and belief systems of all the things you do want instead of what you don't want, chances are if you consciously and subconsciously coherently think and dream about your desires, then you're bound to eventually manifest them into your own personal reality. I genuinely believe that to be the case and throughout the extensive research in writing this book I can assure you all the best and most uplifting scientific experts and spiritual leaders are of the same opinion. So then what if our dreams were one of the purest expressions of our individual spirituality? What if our dreams were a way that our conscious and subconscious mind communicates without any interference from your environment and your ego?

I mean think about it for a second. When you dream at night it doesn't feel as though you're watching an experience, but rather you feel as though you're in it and living it out. For example, at times you may randomly bring up a person from a childhood memory or experience in your dream and then you question, what does that mean? You then delve into some of the meanings and find that there's a message in there for you and then you go on with your day-to-day routines usually dismissing or avoiding its message.

The harsh truth is, who really cares about your dream's meaning if you do nothing with it? If it's a form of you connecting with your spiritual self, if you do absolutely nothing with it and dismiss what you've just dreamt because its message was too good to be true, then what's the point of the dream? Or if you allow it to control you and your day because you're now fearful of its message, then what? Let's be outside the box thinkers! The majority of us go through living our lives based on thoughts and emotions, and most times those thoughts and emotions create our own personal projection of our life, even though at times it may not be exactly what you're experiencing, but rather what you're choosing to experience. Because the way you think dictates the way you feel.

I heard this story about a great Taoist master named Chuang Tzu who once dreamt that he was a butterfly fluttering in the meadows amongst the amazing sunlight and flowers. When he woke he looked distressed and confused, his fellow monks asked him what was wrong and he said he had dreamt he was a butterfly, and that it felt so real. That he was able to smell the flowers and felt the indescribable life force as the sunlight hit his body. His fellow monks said that is a beautiful dream and that they don't know why he would feel distressed and confused. He then said that this dream felt so real that he's now questioning if he is a butterfly dreaming of him now being a man. Or that if he's actually a man dreaming of being that butterfly as they both feel equally as real. The way I see it is who cares why we dream? If either one of those thought processes feel real to us, shouldn't the focus now be for us to create a thought process that feels real about the life we desire to have whether we have it or not? For example if you went through the day genuinely feeling like you're the happiest person in the world and believed it with every inch of your being then chances are nothing could affect you even if you're surrounded by some circumstances that are not favourable. Just like the 'quarks in quantum physics', if you change the way you look at things, the things you look at change.

I guess the intent was again to challenge your thought process into seeing the power that your thoughts and emotions can have on your lives. If you're experiencing your life through thoughts and emotions, then you're more than likely to manifest the projection of those thoughts and emotions. If you can embrace your life as your opportunity to create whatever you desired and set the intention with belief that you genuinely have whatever it is that you're destined for, then both your dreams and your reality would continue to recreate the thoughts and feelings that you already have whatever it is you desired until whatever you desire in life would have no choice but to find you. But before you do that, get out of the way and allow yourself to experience the journey and not try and control it.

When you're able to do that your spirit and body would be in complete coherence, because what you felt inside was able to create the desired environment and when you know that you had a hand in creating that, chances are you'll do it again.

how to sleep better

A great night's sleep begins as soon as you wake up. What you do and don't do throughout the day could be the difference between you sleeping well and cashing in on the myriad of benefits sleep possesses, or not sleeping at all and making yourself susceptible to chronic fatigue and worse. I've taken the liberty in suggesting 6 amazing ways to help you improve how you biologically and physically transition into sleep as well as improve your quality of sleep.

1. **More sun.** The more your body, your face and your eyes are exposed to sunlight and its rich source of nutrients, in particular vitamin D, the more natural serotonin you will produce. Serotonin is a neurotransmitter that regulates everything from mood to sleep. Serotonin is also a precursor to melatonin and melatonin is needed for deep restorative sleep. If you get too much artificial light and not enough sunlight that can have a negative impact on your sleep quality.

2. **Avoid blue light and artificial light before sleeping.** Your smart phones, tablets, laptops, TVs and PCs all emit blue light. Cutting out screen time before you go to bed is the single most effective way to improve your quality of sleep. This blue light disorients your body in its circadian preparation for sleep. If you must use a PC or a smartphone before bed then it may be best to invest in a blue light blocker that you can download from your app store.

3. **Regulate bedroom temperature.** As your body prepares for sleep it automatically drops its body temperature. Scientific research shows that the perfect temperature for sleeping is between 16 and 20 degrees Celsius or 60- and 68-degrees Fahrenheit.

4. **Develop a sleep schedule.** The body is a machine of habit and so it helps if it recognises a regular sleep schedule. That will help create a natural rhythm for the body. The best way to improve sleep patterns is to go to bed between 10 and 10:30 pm as your natural melatonin levels are increased significantly. If you miss this window then the body assumes something isn't right and so it then secretes more cortisol to help you stay awake. That's the reason why at times you could be so tired you do not sleep then you're exhausted at 1 am, but still can't sleep and have become restless. Now your usual reasoning for still being awake is that you're over or past 'being tired'.

5. **Sleep in the dark. Turn off all your lights and make your room completely dark.** The absence of light sends a critical signal to the body that it is time to rest. If there is any light exposure at the wrong times it alters the body's biological mechanisms that regulate your sleep-wake cycles. In particular, the quantity and quality of our sleep hormone melatonin.

This incredible hormone is produced in the brain's pineal gland. It influences our sleep by sending a signal to the brain letting it know that it is time to rest. This signal helps initiate the body's physiological preparations for sleep and then when our muscles begin to relax, feelings of drowsiness increase and our body temperature drops. So if you continue to expose yourself to evening light it'll inhibit the naturally timed rise of your melatonin, which then affects the body's transition into sleep.

6. **Meditation.** This is my favourite of the lot. The idea is to calm your racing mind by spending the last 10 mins before you sleep listening to binaural beats and meditating as they boost REM stimulating regions of the brain and help increase our body's natural secretion of melatonin.

Chronic sleep deprivation has system wide effects on the brain and body. Sleep affects every organ system and can open you up to diseases or exacerbate them. For instance, cancer cells multiply faster the more sleep deprived you are. That's how important sleep is for our overall health and well being and if you don't get this part of the Six Pillars right then there's honestly no point in getting any of the others right. So please make this just as much as a priority to improving your health and well being as you do say nutrition or movement. Again every single one of these pillars are really simple yet profound in the way you live out the rest of your lives.

chapter 12:
the sixth pillar – mindfulness

the mechanics of meditation and the benefits

For thousands of years people have practiced meditation for spiritual, emotional and physical wellbeing. Most people associate meditation with stress management and a means to redefine how they approach their happiness, satisfaction and to help reduce the suffering in their lives.

In a metaphysical sense the goal of meditation is enlightenment and the realisation of the true nature of the mind, and that by being able to improve our level of consciousness that we begin to discover our own individuality.

In short, meditation is really about bringing you back into a state of awareness, a state of consciousness. The most important part of meditating is getting the mechanics right; most people assume that we need to concentrate and be monk-like immediately. I assure you that's not the way it'll end up. This is another reason why meditation can be intimidating to most.

To get it right all you need to do is sit quietly either on the floor or on a chair, make sure you're comfortable and your back slightly erect otherwise you may fall asleep. Close your eyes for a minute or so, don't do anything and what you'll find is that your thoughts will start challenging you. For example, 'I can't believe Dolores said that about me,' or, 'I have to pay bills.'

The idea is to have a mantra or something positive like love or happiness that you recite and as soon as those thoughts come in then simply think of the mantra, don't try and challenge those thoughts. A cool hack to improve your inner attitude is to pretend you're remembering the chosen mantra or listening to it instead of focussing on it, because if you're too fixated and focussed on the mantra it becomes superficial and you won't feel it. The more you feel the mantra, the more significant the mediation will be and there will be times where you will have all these thoughts and your chosen mantra all circling in your mind, and if you experience that that's absolutely fine just keep going. If you slow down your breathing (I don't meant slow down the amount of oxygen you consume; what I mean by that is quite simply breathe longer and slower) and then begin to feel your chosen mantra. When you do, then there will be periods of no thoughts and no mantra, complete calmness. It's a feeling that only can be felt and not described properly, that there is what is classified as pure consciousness and the field of infinite possibilities and pure potential. In this field you become pure creativity and is where you begin to become the architect of your future self where there are no limitations to what you can do, have or be.

A great hack in being able to get into this space of pure creativity is by not wanting or thinking you need to be in that space. Because wanting to be in that space is also a thought and your ego attempting to control the outcome, which goes against the idea of getting into that space.

In short don't focus on the destination, focus on the breathing, the mantra, calming the racing mind and the destination will work itself out. Like anything to get good at meditating you need to practice and make it a regular practice.

Science has started to work out that the benefits to meditating surpass the metaphysical spiritual benefits. Scientists have linked meditation to neuroplasticity. Your first reaction might be how is that possible? How could breathing and meditating effectively do that? As we've previously explained, whenever you engage in a behaviour over and over again, this can lead to changes in your brain, in particular, the way the neurons communicate with each other, through the changes in the new synaptic connections. This is effectively what neuroplasticity means. Other improvements found by researchers are significant improvements on decreasing stress, reducing symptoms associated with depression, anxiety disorders, pain, insomnia, enhanced ability to pay attention, increased quality of life.

what is consciousness?

So what is consciousness, the dictionary definition is that it's basically one's perception or awareness of a thing or circumstance; but could it be more than that, as in could consciousness be all around us?

The source of consciousness has been a fundamental mystery. However, as we advanced in our understanding of the universe and how closely connected we really are, a new picture seems to be emerging and that is that consciousness may just be a field of information that permeates everything including our material world. That beneath the surface of perception is this new phenomenon that you and the world around you is part of something bigger, part of something that you may not really experience every waking moment of your life.

Nassim Haramein, a theoretical and experimental physicist, was attempting to unify physics and ended up with using those same equations to prove that everything in the material world as we know it and space are unified. He went on to state that approximately 100 years ago science had already proved that the space between planets, stars, galaxies or even the space between the atoms in a molecule as well as the space inside the atom itself is not empty. It's made up of energy and so he claims that the fundamental source of all existence and creation is energy.

This revelation isn't anything new, many ancient civilizations believed that everything was energy and this idea hasn't yet been fully explained by modern science. We are learning about these ancient wisdoms in nonconventional ways and finding that they have been present all along. Again, just to clarify, this isn't just some metaphysical woo-woo, it's based on an idea that comes from quantum theory itself. Physicists were testing something that's referred to in quantum theory as 'vacuum fluctuations'. The ultimate finding was that each atom was infinitely dense with energy and that the space inside the atom was not empty at all.

Nassim's theory goes onto suggest what all ancient civilisations already knew and that is that energy is the source of everything that vibrates at a certain frequency. It projects its own reality, that the source of all the material world is mostly space. We are also made out of 99.9999 percent space. This space of energy is full of information and is the medium that connects all things. Nassim was analysing the energy inside the volume of a proton, which is in the nucleus of an atom. He found the amount of energy inside a proton was the exact same mass of the entire universe. So the ultimate finding in his tests was that all the atoms in the whole of the universe are all holographically expressed within one proton, proving that everything is interconnected.

So what this means is that the space between you and I, and the space between all objects is full of energy that we are tapped into all the time. It's all around us, however, for us to become unified consciously with it we must become aware of it. For example, the frequency or radio wave of your favourite radio station is all around us and you can't hear anything until you tune into its frequency. That's the same with this universal consciousness.

But the question remains, how do 'WE' fit into this equation of consciousness? The best way to describe this is that we're like an antenna that is tapping into this infinite well of information. As we walk through space and time we feed it information and so the universe is constantly growing by the information that is fed into it by our beliefs, our experiences, our emotions and our perceptions, and that the reality of life as we know it is part of this space.

As our understanding of this universal consciousness expands we are starting to figure out that everything we've known to be our reality is emerging out of this space. Einstein famously said that an object isn't in space but rather is an extension of space itself. And so you and I are like this extension of the universal subconscious mind feeding back information into it. The question is no longer 'how do we improve our consciousness' but rather 'how do we increase our influence in this highly organised structure of space', seeing that we are always tapped into the universe.

The law of attraction has become this buzzword that no-one can really explain or truly understand, in previous chapters we have highlighted how the unconscious mind works and that it's basically the makeup of our default programs of habits and behaviours. For this to become easier to understand let's just call the space between you and I, the space between everything and everyone, the universal subconscious mind.

We are a highly organised part of the universe where the universal consciousness is expressing itself. Think about it for a second, life as we know it just works; it's as though everything in it from animal to vegetation just works. It's a universal communion where everything just fits in each other's world, the hierarchies of pecking orders, the four seasons, day and night, nothing exists for no reason and that's the same with the universe right down to the atom itself, everything exists from us and for us; this is the fundamental law at the root of all creation. Let that soak in for a second whilst I continue to expand your awareness and allow you to be humbled by how great we truly are and why we really are the creators of our environment.

What is an important distinction is that for anything to have an awareness is that it must have some sort of feedback system. Otherwise how would you know of that object or thing or circumstance? For example, if I were to reach over to touch the wall, unless I get some sort of feedback letting me know that I've touched it, then I would continue to reach forward until I had some sort of visual or sensory feedback of touching the wall. If science teaches us that all space and matter is energy, then maybe the space between you and any object has information being transferred between the particles, kind of like a universal feedback structure through its network, and that is the feedback you receive in your life. That same network allows you to manifest the experiences in your reality, your experiences are a direct result of the information you are transmitting out to this universal intelligence. The universal subconscious mind is feeding information to itself through all our choices, emotions, beliefs and experiences. That's how it grows and becomes more complex and organised, kind of like Google and the internet.

Consciousness is the universe expressing itself through your experiences, perception and beliefs. We're leaving information as we move through space, and by that I mean that your brain and your body is this powerful antenna that is tuned into the universal subconscious frequency tapped into its field of information. The unique thing about consciousness is that not everyone sees the same object from the same perspective, simply because we can only see what we believe to be true. For example let's say that the space between you and I or the space between you and everyone in your home is consciousness and this consciousness was in the form of a phone held up in the centre of the room. Every single one of us would see and describe the phone differently depending on where they were positioned in the room or the house and that's the same with consciousness, although we're all part of the same consciousness. How aware we are is based on how well we're tuned into the frequency of the flow of information available to all of us.

What makes this even more interesting is that unconsciously, we're all feeding a different set of information to this universal subconscious mind and that all the different sets of feedback produce the reality we actually see. We are some of the most sophisticated creations in the universe who are all gathering different bits of information through our experiences and feeding it back to this universal subconscious mind, these sets of feedback information shape our reality and even who we are.

Think about this for a second if God says he made man in his image, and that the makeup of every part of you is based on your cells, and that science proves that the origin of a cell is energy, then effectively the origin of you is also energy. If you're effectively made up of a community of trillions cells that communicate information to each other, then maybe the universe is made up of all the same matter communicating to itself in the same manner and that communication is true consciousness. So if you want to know about the universe, why not just go inside yourself instead of constantly putting our attention on our external environment? We've become so disconnected with ourselves and the world around us and so the purpose of this chapter is to explore the techniques to be able to connect with yourself and the deeper layers to our existence. I pray you allow this new set of knowledge to permeate throughout the rest of your life so that you can finally allow your environment to become an extension of your mind.

You are truly remarkable and capable of infinite possibilities as long as you believe, just remember when **God** created you, you weren't created as a singular person but rather a community of all the trillions of cells, so that you've never been alone and the makeup of who you are is far greater than any other miracle that has ever existed.

how do we increase our awareness and consciousness?

How does consciousness happen and how can we improve our awareness or even better, how can we experience consciousness.

Here is where we highlight that the intention of your journey was to showcase how you are scientifically and spiritually coherent, and that science is the order and spirituality is the unknown and infinite in its information rendering. It is the chaos and mystery of our creation and existence. Science and spirituality is your yin and yang symbol, these two worlds represent the balance between your order and your chaos, just like science will continue to create new order by making breakthrough after breakthrough before diving back into the opportunities of the chaos of what's still 'the spiritually unknown'. Then so will you in life; this path is one that demands that you see the world as you are and not as it is, because when you can appreciate that, you have total control and agency over whatever it is you choose to experience. When you do then you'll inevitably become grateful in every sense of the word and will never allow any moment to go by you before appreciating its lesson and what you can learn and become because of it.

Within each of our brains is the combined activity of billions of neurons that are generating an awareness through a conscious experience, without this feedback or awareness of consciousness there is no world, there is no reality, there is literally nothing for us to remember or appreciate.

Scientists and philosophers from all different disciplines over the past 25 years have created this explosion of information in an attempt to understand the true meaning of consciousness and its direct link with the universe, as the properties of consciousness were being examined inside the brain and body the ultimate finding is that for it to completely be understood it also had to be examined outside the body and as a result this once perceived insoluble mystery of what consciousness is has started to become less of a mystery and more of a revelation because we don't just passively perceive the world, we generate it.

As we've discussed in previous chapters, your brain is constantly trying to figure out your reality and your world, and the only way it can generate its perception is through streams of electrical impulses. Your perception is a process of the informed guesswork of your brain, where your brain combines all of its sensory information with its prior stored data of the beliefs about the way your world is and forms its perception of what has caused your experience or circumstance.

So that when we're faced with a circumstance the brain will use these prior expectations that we've built deeply into any part of our sensory cortex. By adding new predictions to any one of your experiences through new knowledge (semantic memories) or new experiences (episodic memories) we can change what we consciously experience.

By doing so you'll no longer perceive your world, you effectively begin to generate it. Throughout the book we've mentioned and substantiated how thoughts create things and all things are made up of energy that vibrate at certain frequencies, from the tiniest of particles in atoms to the magnitude of the infinite solar system.

So if things create things, and our thoughts are things that have a certain level of energy that vibrates at a certain frequency, then it makes perfect sense that you're connected to the consciousness of the 'universal subconscious mind'; that your perception is confirming your reality and the more you feed your illusions or perceptions into this unified field of consciousness then the more your perception of your reality is intensified, as a result, it continues to manifest as your reality, whether it is negative or positive. The universal subconscious mind does not discriminate where you place this energy, kind of like a satellite navigator system. Once you've set the address of a destination, (by destination I'm referring to your belief system and the vibration of frequency you're transmitting into the consciousness of the unified subconscious mind), the navigator will start to now guide you to your chosen subconscious destination in the quickest and most energy efficient way to your destination. If you deviate, if you try and take a wrong turn by making a conscious choice outside your belief system, the universe will reroute and guide you back to your preferred or chosen destination no matter how many times you deviate or take a wrong turn. In other words if you try and change your life by merely saying it then you'll eventually be rerouted back to your subconscious path of programs and beliefs.

That's exactly the same with your perception and reality. If you believe you don't have enough, you will never have enough; and if you're grateful for what you have, then your life's navigator will continue to re-route you to abundance no matter how many setbacks you experience or detours you take in life. Knowing this, your greatest contribution to humanity is to your own self-realisation, because as you raise your awareness and uplift yourself you immediately uplift everyone else around you.

The best way to increase your awareness and raise your state of consciousness is by meditating.

manifestation

Manifesting is much like the idiom, 'the devil is in the details,' which refers to a mysterious element hidden in the details. That something might seem simple at a first look but will take more time and effort to complete than expected. It is a topic that has become misunderstood. Millions of people globally preach that you either must write it down or be grateful or visualise whatever it is you desire, yet still they don't seem to be able to manifest anything because of the details they miss. Being grateful and writing down what you desire are super important, and so is visualisation, however, we also need the details. We need belief and the feeling that whatever you desire is already yours.

A little story to put the logic of adding as much detail in your visualisation in perspective. My daughter once asked me if she could have money and I said, 'of course you can bubba'. I then gave her 50 cents, she said 'thank you, thank you, but that won't be enough,' I said, 'I gave you money, you never told me how much you wanted!' I then asked her to imagine the difference if she had asked me for $100, then I would know exactly what she wanted. I then said, 'now imagine you asked me for the $100 and that you'd like it given to you as one $50 note, two $20s and a $10 dollar note, that she would be giving me specific details with her request. Then the end result would be that she would get exactly what she asked for to the smallest detail. I then said, 'but there's only one thing, you will get that $100 as long as you were worthy of the desire'. She then asked, 'what do you mean dad?' I said, 'maybe you will have to work for it and earn it.' I then explained to her that's the same with creating the life you desire, that although you may be capable of having a life that's filled with abundance and success that you will still need to be worthy of anything you wish to create. Life may present you with circumstances that will test you and that is only to help prepare you for whatever it is you have asked for.

Visualisation is a great way to help you to become aligned with whatever it is you desire and allow it to become a realisation. Ultimately what I am saying is that to become a master manifester all you need to do is match the *Exact Frequency* of whatever it is you desire. Here's an important tip, if your frequency is too high and by that I mean that you want it so bad that you are scared of missing out on it then you will never be able to manifest it. Equally, if your frequency is too low by telling yourself you'll never have whatever it is you desire then there is absolutely no way you will allow the desire to be realised. Again the key is to match the exact frequency. Let's just say I wish to purchase a brand-new Mercedes; I would immediately visualise the exact car I wish to own. For example, the colour, the style, etc. The next step and by far the most important step is that I would then say to myself, 'I love how I feel when I drive my new car' and feel it with every inch of my being. Deep in the pit of my stomach I would feel the feelings of driving my new car on the road. How the steering wheel feels in my hands, how the wind feels in my hair and the sun on my skin. In those moments I would feel so happy and grateful for the car, I would then say that *'I am so happy and grateful for my new Mercedes'* and then let it go, let the universe do its thing but remain in the vibrational frequency of having that Mercedes. Visualisation is an exceptional tool that will allow you to experience and feel the sensation of being in the vibrational frequency of your desire.

In the end no matter how you see your life, the **objective truth** threading in each of the chapters has showcased that you genuinely are the creator of your own reality. The point here is that just as much as you can manifest your desires by being in the vibrational frequency of what you do want, that you also can manifest the life that you don't want by being in that victim mindset and repeatedly expressing that. Whenever you feel like life is constantly throwing you curveballs, remember that life is only sending you the circumstances that are in direct alignment of the frequency that is resonating with you. What I'm saying is that life isn't testing you, it's not against you, it's not challenging you; it's only responding to you and preparing you for whatever you asked for.

Your life is happening around you and you're participating in it through your awareness and through your conversations and more importantly perceptions. You are inevitably attracting whatever it is you are unconsciously concluding. Unfortunately most people keep recreating what they don't want and that's based on this evolutionary feedback system that keeps highlighting what we don't want. As I said earlier, *the law of substitution says that what I tell myself is what I think about and focus on.* So if your thought pattern is reflecting the frequency of things you cannot have, then you will never have them, because we habitually say to ourselves things like 'I was born that way' or 'I'll never stop being like that' or 'I've always been like that'.

The last message here is that in order to draw the things you desire to you, all you really need to do is meet the vibration of whatever it is you desire, you can't be too low by wanting it badly enough you fear never getting it or too high for example overly excited. Once you've matched the frequency and the belief the last step is to let the universe do its thing. Visualisation is the best way to help you find and match the frequency of whatever it is you desire.

meditation challenge

If meditation has been something you've cringed at or have been intimidated by, then let's start with just 5 minutes of meditation every day and see if you don't notice the profound differences after a month. That's all I am asking. That you please commit to this for only a month. If it's not for you then that's fine but give it a genuine go. Apply all of this newfound knowledge you've acquired so far and add the desire and intent of changing your life for the better and I assure you that it'll end up being something you end up relying on to keep you balanced.

Just 5 minutes a day to be mindful to help you find your inner voice and allow it to guide you; preferably in the morning if you can, that it will help set the pace of the day, that it will help keep you focussed and poised and allow you to be in control and dictate the outcomes of your day no matter what variable will present itself. Most importantly, you won't feel as though you're chasing the day due to having a bad start.

The secret to genuinely quieting your racing mind and listening to your inner self is to 'Not' try and control your thoughts and that when they challenge you, that you don't entertain them. They will move on over all by themselves. The more times you repeat this the easier this process will get and there will come a time when you'll know and feel like you're in the place of complete silence and in control. You will be in that space where there is infinite potential, in the place of pure creativity, and is when you should implement the visualisations, the gratitude, and the belief of the environment you wish to experience, that is when the experience will have absolutely no choice but to find you. This might sound easy and it is, but you'll need practice. So just sit in complete silence, get out of your own way, don't allow your ego to try and control the moment. This process is not just useful to manifest, it's equally as powerful if you have a question you are unsure of. If you set the intention and then ask the question you would love answered, I assure you the answer will come to you when you're able to calm your racing mind and listen. That is the exact same process I used when I was writing this book every time I felt stuck, I would ask the question I needed answered to the universal subconscious mind. I would then meditate and as soon as I quieted the mind and was in an altered state of consciousness the answers would come to me every time. Just like anyone, I too experienced thoughts that challenge me. In those moments I simply observed those thoughts as if they were on a conveyor belt and then select the thoughts or topics I'd like to focus on and by doing so I would eventually find the missing pieces to the topics I was struggling with. The reality of our lives is that we pay attention to all the stimulus in our surrounding environment that we've neglected to take the time to pay attention to the 'Self'.

Knowing what you now know, don't you think that it's about time you focussed on cashing in on all the amazing gifts you were created for by finally connecting with yourself and genuinely getting to know who you really are, rather than who you think you are. Or worse, who you've been told you are. Embrace this challenge as a chance to grow, and that's when you finally meet yourself. When you do, then all I ask is that you be me for someone else and introduce them to themselves, not just by meditating but by utilising all of these Six Pillars.

Now, to be the change you wish to see in the world!

bringing it all together

Throughout the journey of the book the consistent message in all of the pillars, from the sounds we hear to the thoughts we think, from the food we consume to the air we breathe, from the way we move to how we sleep, everything was *Energy* that vibrates at a certain frequency. Everything is energy, frequency and vibration. The idea of this journey was to get you to appreciate the fact that when you drink a glass of water that you realise that you're not just drinking water, that you're adding life in the form of energy, or that when you eat your next meal that the purpose of the nutrient rich foods is to improve your internal lifeforce. With this newfound knowledge you begin to connect with everything in your environment, where you begin to have this newfound appreciation and connect with all the building blocks that are created for you, rather than continue to consume anything that would suck the life force from you.

The best thing about the *Six Pillars* is that they highlight that the most profound impacts in the way you overcome any of your environmental assaults that affect your mental, physical and emotional health are the simplest things and in no way need to be complicated.

The release of this book at this present time couldn't have been any more critical as we've now lost our way and are in an era of uncertainty, We've lost sight of what our core principles are and the make-up of who we are. We've kind of lost our identity and have transcended a lot of our evolutionary programming. For example, if we were hungry we would have to expend energy to get energy and hunt for our food and forage for berries. Whereas nowadays we simply log into Uber Eats and the food is delivered to your front door without even expending any calories. So although we have made so many technological advancements, we genuinely should express extreme caution in designing these advancements to serve us rather than work against us.

I have no doubt you are ready to finally create the change you've desired. I mean you've committed yourself to reading this entire book, that's got to stand for something significant. Especially if you're one that never seems to finish anything they start. I ask that your new personal mantra become 'Just do this, Get it done'. No more fussing around or looking for some external source of motivation. All you've ever needed was a clearer picture, so with this newfound clarity create your new cognitive script. The new mental shortcut that will keep you focussing on the habits that will finally allow you to experience the world you desire. The easiest way to initiate change is to start by changing your habits; it's actually quite that simple. As you now know your life is a sum total of your habits, the definition of a habit is a behaviour that has been repeated that many times it's basically now on autopilot, to where you do these things without thinking about them. Your brain sets these repeated behaviours on auto pilot because energy is the most important commodity that all of life needs to survive, which obviously includes your brain and body. Your brain is constantly figuring out ways to save energy. Habits just so happen to be an exceptional way of conserving energy, so the brain begins to form neurological connections and embed them as your preferred pattern when it recognises that you turn to these newfound habits all the time.

Once you've set the intention to change write it down, remember to write it down, make it real, let yourself and the universal subconscious mind, God if you will, know that you are serious this time, that no matter what is now thrown at you, you'll just shut up and get it done. Don't try and perfect it, just do it! In medical and scientific research documents that were assessing the performance of their test subjects that implemented quality versus quantity, the general consensus was that all the test subjects that did not focus on perfecting the task, but rather just got it done, had a better overall outcome in performance. There was this example I heard James Clear use, who is the author of 'Atomic Habits', that puts the concept of *'Just get this done and don't worry about perfecting it immediately'* in perspective. There was this photography professor who ran an experiment with his students. He split the class into two groups and asked the first group to take as many photographs as possible. He gave them a quota of a hundred pictures which would give them an A, and if it was less than the grade it would also be less and relevant to the quantity of photographs. The second group were only asked to submit one photograph, just one photograph, however, there was one condition; it had to be the most perfect photograph they could ever imagine. The result was that the group who submitted quantity had a higher-grade average then the group who took only one perfect photograph. You see whilst the quantitative group were now experimenting and learning and making mistakes they would eventually come across a great photograph whereas whilst the quality group were too busy wasting time theorising and trying to figure out what was perceived to be a great photograph, they ended up submitting something that was average at best.

building better habits

Inch by Inch, Anything's a Cinch

Changing your life might seem like it's a little too late for you or the picture you desire might seem overwhelming to attain; I assure you if you focus on the micro habits instead of focussing on the final destination it'll be a more practical concept to implement and one that will see you not overwhelm yourself. My suggestion is that you 'Start small', don't over complicate this process, it's the small habit changes that progressively over a lengthy period of time will have the most profound impact on transforming our lives, for example the captain of a ship turns the wheel and navigates 1 degree off course. Immediately, you wouldn't notice the difference but over 300 miles you could be way off course and it's the same thing with the 1 percenters in life that you would usually overlook.

So by changing from tap water to a quality source of water and drinking optimal amounts every day you end up noticing the improvements over the long run. Equally, when you work out, you won't notice the changes immediately even though in the short term you will feel the positive effects of the endorphin rush. The long-term results will be far superior to the short-term ones.

Habits that are immediately rewarding and satisfying are more than likely to be repeated and this is why it's important to keep the tasks simple so that you never regress once you've set your intention. *Atomic Habits*, by James Clear, highlights the fact that many people think they lack motivation to start something when all they really lack is structure; and so the inevitable is that you wake up in the morning questioning whether or not you feel like working out, for example. If you set yourself a structure of when you will work out, where and how, you effectively take the decision making out of it.

What I am suggesting is that although there has been so much you've taken in and learnt about yourself throughout your journey of the book, that whilst you start to process the events of your life, and process the emotions you've experienced and held onto, why not just start with creating the intention, a vision and then a structured plan to get you on your way? This is in no way about you dictating the outcomes of your life but giving you the tools in order to help you create the right habits so that your desired outcome will have no choice but to be in your life. This way it's less overwhelming for you whilst you still process your past events and experiences, remember that although you may have to forgive things you don't want to or release emotions you've been identifying yourself with, that life starts now, in the present moment, and that once you process the past and initiate the vision of the future and then act on it, you effectively become the captain of your ship.

> 'True wisdom is when you can visit a past experience and have no associated emotions attached to it.'
> ~ Joe Dispenza

Our environment usually dictates our behaviour or our actions whether it is an impulse, a trigger or social pressures of any sort, so instead of being the victim of your environment you become the architect by implementing and designing the environment that will allow you to make better choices and have better behaviours that are easier to sustain.

Many of our habits, both positive or negative, are formed because our environment is repeatedly allowing us to continue to focus on them; and so they become our default program and the new norm. The point is that it's virtually impossible, or at least it's an uphill climb to stick to any new habits you desire if you remain in the environment that allowed your negative habits to manifest. If you don't believe me then try it, you might be able to overcome temptation and have the willpower a few times, but eventually you will cave in. That's because your subconscious programming is a million times more powerful than your conscious mind and it will test you as soon as you desire and initiate any type of program that goes against any of its preferred automatic programs. And rightly so it should. Think about it. For the past 10, 20 or 30 years you have been oblivious and in no way present, focussing on all the things you don't want. Your subconscious ran on autopilot, keeping you alive by creating programs it saw as your repeated and preferred habits, all in an attempt to conserve energy and keep you alive. And now you think you can take over and captain your vessel again. Remember, your vessel needs a commander and so you have to prove yourself to your subconscious and show it that you're genuinely back in charge before it believes you and allows you adopt the new habits of desire.

Remember that any desire that you aspire to achieve will need the golden rule of repetition, and so the bigger the desired change you wish to create, the more times you'll need to repeat it. The truth is once you forge these new micro habits into your neurological pathways via your synaptic connections then they will no longer feel like a repetition as you now begin to identity with it. This is why it's imperative that you to do the work, no matter what comes up make the new habits your daily priority and repeat them.

A very important point that will help you create the new habits of desire is that we tend to repeat the behaviours that we like. Figure out a way of bringing some sort of reward into the present moment of the habit. The reason why is that long term habits can become boring and may lead to losing motivation. For example, if getting a beach body is one change you desire, then going to the gym has delayed consequences and results which sees most people tend to give up as there really isn't an immediate reward or outcome. The best way to attack this potential setback is to create short term rewards so that you can enjoy the moment.

It can be overwhelming thinking that you need to change everything in your life to become someone new; and so if you can focus on the micro changes it will improve your level of consistency and repetition. I promise you that there will come a time where you will become who you're destined to be and that you will change your outcomes, your results and your identity.

IIIIIIIIIIIIIIIIIIIIIIIIIIIIIIIIIIIIIIIIIIIIIIIIIIIIIIIII

'The actions you take provide
evidence of who you are, and the
things you do once or twice fade
away and the things you do day in
day out end up providing the
evidence of who you are.'
~ James Clear

IIIIIIIIIIIIIIIIIIIIIIIIIIIIIIIIIIIIIIIIIIIIIIIIIIIIIIIII

implementation of intention

I am in no way promoting a 12-week program. What we are actually doing is setting our long-term goals and then shifting the focus onto the micro habits that will allow us to reverse engineer and attain the achievement we desire, one habit at a time. By applying a shorter and more manageable time frame it will almost guarantee that you will succeed, because as we discussed earlier, habits that are immediately rewarding are more likely to be repeated. So set the habits in place you can achieve and every time you revisit this agreement, simply implement a better variation of what it is you previously achieved so that you continue to progress and eventually allow your environment to become an extension of all your desires. Again that can only eventuate by actively living out the life you desire in a way that you already have it.

Test and compare your progress every time you complete the 12-week period, don't ever settle, keep setting higher standards with every 12-week agreement. If you're anything like me *('Extremely competitive')* then this will make you become obsessive about improving and competing with your past self. Monitor and track your progress and then make the adjustments needed to improve every 12 weeks. The more times you commit to this the better you'll get at it, until it is no longer an agreement but rather a newfound part of your everyday life.

Make this your initial agreement; During the next 12 weeks I _____ will partake in making each of the Six Pillars a regular habit, I will consume the optimal amount of water, I will nourish my body, I will be active and make the most of all the benefits associated with movement and an active lifestyle, I will no longer allow stress to control and dictate my actions and most importantly I will focus on sleeping between 10 pm and 6 am every day.

Then sign your intention letter to yourself and hang it up all over your house. By doing so you'll inevitably increase your odds of success in being able to transform life as you know it, and this once perceived idea of assuming you needed some sort of motivation, will no longer be a focal point as your new realisation will be that all you've ever needed was a clearer picture of who identify yourself to be, or aspire to be like was to simply have a plan.

Setting the intention or desire is critical, however, to complete all the components that go into the transformational holy trinity you also need an action and faith. This pyramid principle all feeds off each other, the *intention* sets your *desires*, your *desires* can only be driven by *faith*, *faith* in yourself and more importantly *faith* in the fact that you already have whatever it is you desire.

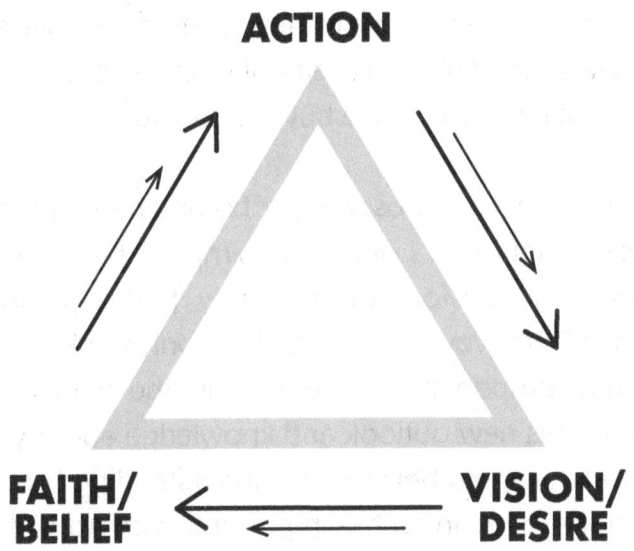

This all feeds into each other
and intensifies itself
every time a cycle is complete.

Initially having faith that you have whatever it is you desire might be a little hard for you to digest as you may feel a little foolish, however it is such an important piece to this puzzle as it becomes the preview to your future aspiration. By having the faith that you already have whatever it is you desire will reflect in the way you behave the rest of the day; you will start to gravitate towards better behaviours that marry with the belief that you have or that you will have whatever it is you're working towards. That now will drive you and intensify the desire even more, which now intensifies your faith and inevitably your actions and this newfound cyclic pattern will keep feeding into itself until this newfound desire will have no choice but to find you.

The reason why most people fail and regress is the lack of action, it's quite that simple which makes this 'holy transformational trinity' power pyramid essential for your success and will only work if each of the components are treated with the highest priority. This new outlook and knowledge about your past habits and behaviours, understanding how to change them and more importantly how to sustain them, will have the most profound impact on how you view yourself, which reflects in your new habits and behaviours to the point where your dreams and aspirations will always be bigger than your problems.

Remember don't be scared to fail, you're not meant to go through life unscathed and unweathered, and your journey may not always be the way you imagined it. I can't promise you'll never be hurt, however, if you look at each perceived failure with a growth mindset and see it as an opportunity to grow then I assure you, you will live out the rest of your life without regret.

Remember everything you go through is God's way of preparing you for what you've asked for.

about the author

My journey began around 20 years ago when I began one of my degrees in medical and health sciences. A few years later, something happened that would make me re-evaluate everything I was doing.

About 16 years ago, I saw a specialist for chronic arthritis in my knees. I was in my early twenties, a fit guy, and here I was with this debilitating condition. All I could think was if my knees feel this bad now, what will it be like in 10-, 20-, or 30-years' time? I was more than a little worried. How would this affect my health, my career in health and well-being? I needed someone to help me. To give me some answers. Guide me to a better place.

That didn't happen. Instead, I was treated like a number. It was like the doctor ticked a set of boxes and those boxes became the total of my condition and who I am.

The summary prognosis was invasive surgery. I believed there had to be a better way. However, that experience spurred me on. It made me want to learn more about my knees, my condition, my body, myself. Maybe a little stubbornly, I also wanted to prove this doctor wrong.

MY JOURNEY

I took all the learning from my various degrees and embarked on a journey that would take me even deeper, into areas such as exercise physiology, sports coaching, Heart Math, neuro-linguistic programming (NLP), nutrition including metabolic type, educational kinesiology, physical therapy and rehabilitation, behavioural psychology and neuroscience. I became a sponge for knowledge about the human body.

Each discovery felt like switching on a light in a dark room, only to discover another door to walk through, another light to switch on, and more things to learn. I started to appreciate the remarkable complexity of the human body and the deep connection between the body and the mind, the BodyMind.

I began to develop a holistic approach to helping people attain health and wellbeing, but more than that, empowering them to do it for themselves.

Giving people the knowledge and tools to make better choices and to make sustainable change in their lives. It has not always been a conventional journey. Sometimes we draw inspiration from unlikely sources.

Since starting my business Body By Michael (BBM) 15 years ago, I've worked with athletes, bodybuilders, the elderly, children, the lean and the obese, the full gamut. Each person was unique, and each has taught me something. What inspires me is when I see someone I'm working with changing their outlook, their energy, and their life. These breakthrough moments make everything worthwhile. It's why I do what I do.

WE ARE ALL INDIVIDUALS

One such instance was when I helped a woman who weighed 140 kilograms lose weight. At first, she was too afraid to visit me. She would wait until my facility was closed because she didn't want anyone to see her. She was self-conscious; she hid from others, and she hid from herself. I told her, just come along and have a look at the program, no charge, just give me a chance. Let me try to help you. Together, we unlocked something inside of her. We found the key to the prison she had constructed in her mind. The mind is wonderfully powerful; it can set us free or imprison us. This woman was obese not because she didn't slavishly obey some calories in/calories out mantra or didn't exercise until she passed out; she was obese because she was locked into a mindset that made obesity her default choice. Since then she has lost around 70 kilograms and has maintained her new weight.

More importantly, she cast off the beliefs that led to her destructive behaviour, the behaviour that created her reality. We transformed her thinking from being about diet and exercise, to nutrition and movement. She was no longer disciplining her body by counting calories; she was nourishing her body. The drudgery of exercise shifted to the liberation of movement. That's a subtle but profound shift.

Another more personal moment of awakening for me came in the form of my beautiful nephew. He was diagnosed with autism, which rocked my sister's world. My heart ached for both of them. I saw my sister's struggle to make sense of how she would go forward; what kind of life could she give her son? What I noticed too was that so much of the expert medical opinion she was being given focussed on treating autism as a problem. I watched my nephew move. I watched him eat. I looked at him as an individual. This marvellous, miraculous human being.

We started to shift the narrative away from seeing his autism as a problem to being a blessing. He is not me. He is not my sister. He is his own person. What foods helped him? What spaces made him comfortable? What triggered negative responses? How could we help this person be his very best?

We no longer let autism define him. Autism was a detail in his picture, not the whole landscape. We pulled back the lens. We changed our perspective. We created a new reality that respected him as an individual on his own journey. The holistic approach to health, working with special needs children opened me up to new ways of thinking.

It made me reflect more deeply on the cycle of thought that shapes who we are and who we can be. Perspective creates perception, perception creates belief, belief creates behaviour, behaviour creates an experience, that experience creates your reality, which then creates your perspective. This cycle affects us physically, mentally, and emotionally.

All these elements feed into one another. To make sustainable change, we have to take a holistic approach to our health and wellbeing. We have to dispel the quick-fix myths too often glamorised in the media. We have to stop focussing on washboard abs and vanity metrics. No two people are alike. We are individuals with different needs, different capacities, and different goals.

The aim of this book is to equip people with knowledge and empower them to choose the very best path for their journey to health and wellbeing, to help them become the very best they can be, physically, mentally, and emotionally; to give them a blueprint for a healthier, more fulfilled life.

breakout

breakout

Appendix A:

MICHAEL'S SIX PILLARS SUMMARY

Movement:

We were created and designed to move. We are opportunistic movers, streamlined and designed for multi-joint, multiplane, dynamic movement against the force of gravity over distance. We are a system of integrated systems that only operate best in the presence of movement.

No longer be intimidated by exercise and enjoy the myriad of benefits associated with movement!

Nutrition:

The oversimplified 'calories in vs calories out' theory has been glamorised without any real biochemistry taken into consideration or no real knowledge of what's happening intrinsically. For example, 1) how different foods are used up in the body, 2) what metabolic advance you could have by eating certain foods while avoiding others, and 3) the effect they have on the body.

Understanding this component makes all the difference in creating sustainable change.

The word Nourish, derived from the 1200's is Latin for 'to care for' food is meant to have healing and repair properties instead of being the cause of all the man made Dis-eases.

Breathing:

3 seconds without oxygen and our cells will die, all of our biological systems are dependent on oxygen to function, although the benefits to breathing are far more comprehensive than just staying alive. This chapter will open you up to a brand-new way of appreciating better breathing.

Correct breathing provides your cells with oxygen and helps your body absorb nutrients; it stimulates the lymphatic system to get rid of toxins. So if you breathe shallow, your cells are receiving fewer nutrients and your lymphatic system will become a liability.

Hydration:

Water, referred to as the messenger of God by world renowned scientists. Throughout this chapter you'll find out why, apart from the fact that majority of you is made of water! If you regulate your water intake and work on prioritizing it during your day, you can contribute to improving your weight loss while also investing in your overall health wellbeing.

Sleep:

Besides its myriad health benefits, sleep is an integral factor in losing weight and feeling good. So, why don't we take advantage of the easiest part of losing weight?

Focus on the natural sleep wave patterns that occur between 10 PM and 6 AM to help maximise your fat burning potential. During that time, our bodies go through neurogenic and hormonal repair cycles, which are imperative for growth and tissue repair.

Mindfulness:

For thousands of years people would associate mindfulness with meditation in spiritual practices, however the benefits are far more superior to that, besides it being amazing for stress management and to help reduce the suffering in your life. The chapter outlines how significant you become in being able to control the outcomes in your life when you can connect with yourself and the world around you by being in the moment.

This doesn't mean that it can only be achieved by only meditating.

Appendix B

FOUR-WEEK FASTING AND MEAL PLAN STRUCTURE

1. Fasting:
Nominate an 8-hour window to eat that suits you, your lifestyle and requirements and circumstance. For example 8am - 4pm or 12pm - 8pm.

2. Portion Control:
Keep in mind that there is no limit to how much food you can consume. The idea of portion control is to reduce the amount of food the stomach will consume in any one given meal. This will work out to your advantage in your free days.

This will make sense when you experience how quickly you'll become satiated when you have free reign to eat whatever it is your heart desires.

The portion sizes are your fist size at the ratio of:
- 1 Protein:
- 1 Legume:
- 1 Vegetable/Salad or 1 Protein:
- 1 Vegetable:
- 1 Salad

- 1 Protein:
- 1 Salad:
- 1 Salad or 1 Protein:
- 1 Vegetable:
- Vegetable

(as per the food chart in Appendix C)

From Monday to Friday you are to remain on that program until midday on Saturday. Then you are free to eat as you please as long it's not processed or any foods that can sit on the shelf for weeks without going off.

This is now your free time 12pm Saturday – 6pm Sunday night, no fasting throughout that period.

3. Water:

Please consume 3% of your bodyweight in quality drinking water (strictly no tap water please). During the fasting period no sugary drinks are allowed, no drinks other than green tea, or herbal teas, black coffee and water.

4. With the exercise you are to do the workout *first thing in the morning* using the 20/20/20 principle where you pick one exercise (for example skipping or star jumps) and you go as hard as you can for 20 seconds. Then you rest for 20 seconds and repeat that 20 times please!

Appendix C

FOUR-WEEK FOOD LIST
ProjectYou.tv Lose 10kgs in 4 Weeks Food List

	THE DONT'S
QUALITY SOURCE OF PROTEIN	lunch meats, hot dogs or any other processed meats, shark, swordfish, orange (in moderation, as these fish are extremely high in mercury)
FATS & OILS	canola oil, cottonseed oil, Crisco hydrogenated oils, fake butter options, soybean oil, vegetable oil
NUTS & SEEDS	roasted, salted or sugar-coated nuts and seeds
DAIRY	all commercial dairy products including butter and NO MARGARINE
VEGETABLES	NO potatoes or starchy vegetables until your designated day off
BEVERAGES (FASTED STATE)	NO SUGARY DRINKS. For example, Gatorade, Vitamin Water V, Redbull, Coca Cola or any soft drinks, even if they're zero calories or sugar.
BEVERAGES (NON-FASTED STATE)	NO SUGARY DRINKS. For example, Gatorade, Vitamin Water V, Redbull, Coca Cola or any soft drinks, even if they're zero calories or sugar.
LEGUMES OR GRAINS	No rice or breads until designated day off and if you must have bread choose sourdough please.
SUGAR (ONLY IN THE NON-FASTED STATE)	

THE DO'S

bass, beef, bison, buffalo, bream, chicken, clams, lobster, duck, eggs, emu, goose, lamb, mackerel, mahi-mahi, mussels, mutton, organic meats, oysters, pork, snapper, salmon, sardines, scallops, tuna, trout, turkey, veal, venison, wild game

avocado, avocado oil (cold pressed), back fat, chicken fat, coconut butter, coconut milk, coconut oil, duck fat, flax oil (cold pressed), palm oil, tallow, sesame oil (cold pressed)

almonds, almond butter, Brazil nuts, cashews cashew butter, ABC butter (almond, Brazilian nut and cashew), chestnuts, flax seeds, hazel nuts, macadamia nuts, peanuts, pecan, pine nuts, pumpkin seeds, sesame seeds, sunflower seeds, walnuts. *Note: raw and natural is always preferred.*

organic butter, organic cheeses or cheese made with non-animal rennet, raw or organic cultured dairy products, for example kefir, yoghurt, organic milk

artichoke, asparagus, beetroot, broccoli, Brussel sprouts, cabbage, carrots, cauliflower, coriander, collards, cucumber, dandelion, eggplant, endive, spring onion, kale, lettuce, mushrooms, greens of all sorts, onion, parsley, capsicum/peppers, radish, sea vegetables, spinach, Swiss chard, tomatoes, turnip, yellow squash, zucchini

Consume ½ your bodyweight in ounces of quality drinking water if you weigh yourself in pounds, or 3% of your bodyweight if you weigh yourself in kilograms.
Herbal teas and black coffee with no sugar

Consume ½ your bodyweight in ounces of quality drinking water if you weigh yourself in pounds or 3% of your bodyweight if you weigh yourself in kilograms. Coconut water, fresh vegetable juices (fruit juices are allowed only on your designated day off). Herbal teas and coffee with milk is fine.

All lighter coloured beans are preferred, chickpeas, buckwheat, quinoa, millet.

Stevia, maple syrup, unheated/heated honey
(all of these in moderation please)

www.ingramcontent.com/pod-product-compliance
Lightning Source LLC
Chambersburg PA
CBHW010243010526
44107CB00061B/2662